Christian Thought Year 2
A Level Revision Guide

OCR H573/3

2016 Specification

Daniella Dunsmore & Peter Baron

Published by Active Education

www.peped.org

First published in 2017

ISBN: 9781973520429

©Active Education Ltd

Cartoons used with permission © Becky Dyer

All images © their respective owners

Links, reviews, news and revision materials available on www.peped.org

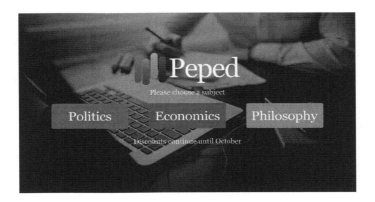

www.peped.org website allows students and teachers to explore Philosophy of Religion and Ethics through handouts, film clips, presentations, case studies, extracts, games and academic articles.

Pitched just right, and so much more than a text book, here is a place to engage with critical reflection whatever your level. Marked student essays are also posted.

Contents

'The unexamined life is not worth living' Socrates

About this Guide

The OCR 2016 specification H573 has posed some challenges for teacher and student, and for this reason this guide represents the foundation of a new approach to revision which integrates elements of the Peped project.

- The textbooks have produced their own interpretation of the specification, in the sense of **ADDITIONAL AUTHORS** and ideas, which you don't necessarily need to adopt or follow. They have overlaid an additional discussion of philosophers and philosophical ideas in order to **EVALUATE** the fairly brief content of the specification. So it is essential you understand that you will be examined on knowledge and content alone - and you can use whoever you like to evaluate and criticise this content. You will notice that, for example, **BUTLER** and **NEWMAN** remain in this guide (under Section 5, Conscience) even though only Freud and Aquinas are named in the specification, because you need to bounce the ideas of some different philosophers off the named ones. **You should download and print out now a hard copy of the relevant pages of the specification**.

- The three papers need to be integrated to produce what is called **SYNOPTIC** insight. This literally means elements of the three papers that can be 'seen together' or linked up. For example, Kant's **MORAL ARGUMENT** (Philosophy of Religion) links and to his ethics which links to **HICK**'s universal **PLURALISM** (Christian Thought) as Hick is greatly inspired by Kant. The Peped website shows additional ways to integrate the three papers and there will be a **REVISION** section accessible for those who have this guide showing you how to increase your synoptic understanding. **Those**

who have this guide should have a head-start, but you need to supplement it with other ideas and sample answers.

- Our approach is to teach for **STRUCTURES OF THOUGHT**. These are given by the mind-maps in this guide. Notice these are not free-for-all scatter diagrams but are structures that move from worldview through to conclusion. And the same structure will be there in the website and in the other revision materials - with creative and hopefully enjoyable tasks you can use to test your understanding. You need to run with this concept of structures, and if you do so, I believe your chances of an A grade or A* will be greatly enhanced. They remind us to reason from **WORLDVIEW** and assumptions through to a conclusion that follows.

Peped represents a community of teachers who are talking and testing things all the time, in a great co-operative conversation.

We are talking with two aims in mind: to put the 'wow!' back into Religious Studies and make sure hard concepts are made crystal clear and then applied through everyday culture.

Even Augustine's doctrine of original sin or Kant's categorical imperative have echoes in our culture today.

And ultimately we'll only be good philosophers and A* candidates if we have learned to read our culture and make sure our answers are full of relevance as well as crystal clarity and razor-sharp evaluation.

For Peped revision events please go to the website and look under 'Events', and you can meet us in person!

Religious Pluralism and Theology

Background

Christianity has always existed alongside other religions. In its growth out of Judaism, Christians had to decide the extent to which they would continue with beliefs and practices of others, and what was it that was going to make them distinctively Christian. The question of whether other religions contain valuable truths remains, as well as the extent to which Christians can be seen to have a unique relationship with God. Issues within religious pluralism and society also arise, for example, should Christians work to convert others or is it possible for non-Christians to achieve salvation too.

Specification

At A level, you will need to explain and evaluate the teaching of contemporary Christian theology of religion on exclusivism, inclusivism, and pluralism. You need to show knowledge and understanding of:

1. The view that only Christianity fully offers the means of salvation

2. The view that although Christianity is the normative means of salvation, 'anonymous' Christians may also receive salvation

3. The view that there are many ways to salvation, of which Christianity is one path (OCR A Level in Religious Studies Specification, 2016, p. 36)

Key Terms

EXCLUSIVISM: the view that only one religion offers the full means of salvation

INTER-FAITH DIALOGUE: discussing religious beliefs between members of different religious traditions, with an intention of reaching better understanding

THEOLOGY OF RELIGION: a branch of Christian theology that considers the relationship between Christianity and other world religions from a Christian perspective

INCLUSIVISM: the view that although one's own religion sets the standard (is 'normative') for means of salvation, those who accept its fundamental principles may also attain salvation

PLURALISM: the view that there are several means of salvation through different religious traditions

PARTICULARISM: another name for exclusivism, meaning that salvation can only be found in one particular way

VATICAN II: the Second Vatican Ecumenical Council, held from 1962 to 1965 to deliberate the place of the Catholic Church in the modern world

NOUMENA: a Kantian term to describe reality as it really is, unaffected by the human mind

PHENOMENA: a Kantian term to describe reality as it seems to us, filtered by

Structure of Thought - Religious Pluralism

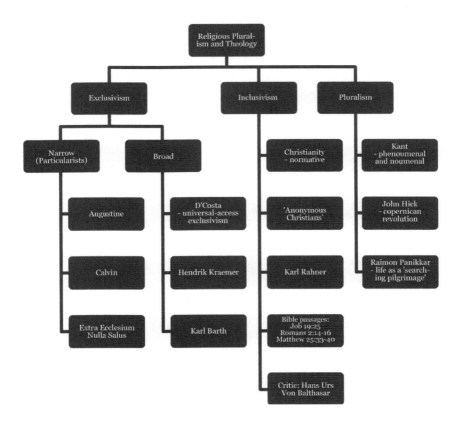

Christian Teaching on Exclusivism

EXCLUSIVISM is the belief that only Christianity offers the means of salvation. It comes from the belief that Jesus is 'the' way, not 'a' way to salvation. Another word for exclusivism is **PARTICULARIST**.

Christ's **SACRIFICE** was **UNIQUE**. Salvation can only reach those who hear the gospel and respond to this with faith. A sign of this acceptance is **BAPTISM**.

NARROW EXCLUSIVISM is the belief that salvation is possible only for those of a particular Christian denomination (Baptist, Catholic, Lutheran, Anglican). **AUGUSTINE** and **CALVIN** are examples of **PARTICULARISTS**. They believed God only elects – through grace - a small number of Christians for salvation. **Catholics** believe there is no salvation outside of the Church – **EXTRA ECCLESIAM NULLA SALUS**. The Catholic view has been considered less narrow since **LUMEN GENTIUM** – "many elements of sanctification and of truth are found outside of its visible structure" (1964).

BROAD EXCLUSIVISM is the belief that salvation is possible for all who accept Christ, regardless of denomination. Other religions may contain some truth, but not enough for salvation. Gavin **D'COSTA** asserted **UNIVERSAL-ACCESS EXCLUSIVISM –** that salvation is possible after death.

1 TIMOTHY 2:3-4 supports this – "this is good, and pleases God our Saviour, who wants all people to be saved and to come to a knowledge of the truth".

HENDRIK KRAEMER – The Christian Message in a Non-Christian World. Kraemer was part of the **ECUMENICAL MOVEMENT** aiming to bring different Christian denominations together. Worked among missionaries in non-Christian countries, spreading the message that salvation could only be achieved by converting to Christianity. We should evaluate religions **HOLISTICALLY** to see if 'as a whole', the religion accepts Christ's salvation or not.

KARL BARTH – Church Dogmatics. Emphasised the importance of Christ for salvation. Humans cannot achieve salvation on their own. Presents **'THEOLOGY OF THE WORD'** – God can only be known where He chooses to reveal this knowledge through His Word – through Christ's life, death, and resurrection; through the Bible and through Church teaching. Revelation is always God's choice. **CHRIST** is the **FULLY UNIQUE** way God has chosen to reveal himself and so is the only fully reliable way of gaining knowledge of God.

Christian Teaching on Inclusivism

INCLUSIVISM is a middle path between exclusivism and pluralism. Christianity is a **NORMATIVE** means of salvation but **'ANONYMOUS'** Christians may also receive salvation (Karl **RAHNER**).

Salvation can be reached by people who turn to Christ in the **AFTERLIFE**. Salvation is possible for those who follow God sincerely, albeit in a wrong religious context. Truth in other religions could be from Christ – even if they do not recognise this.

KARL RAHNER – Christianity sets the **STANDARD** by which other religions should be measured. An **OMNIBENEVOLENT** God should be able to offer salvation to those who have not been able to freely accept Christ. Christianity holds the truth, but people can follow Christ unknowingly. People who do not know Christ can still have a relationship with God – e.g. **JOB 19:25**. Such people are called **ANONYMOUS CHRISTIANS**.

HENDRIK KRAEMER - disagreed with Rahner. **NON-CHRISTIAN RELIGIONS** were **CULTURAL CONSTRUCTS**, not responses to God's revelation through Christ.

The **BIBLE** can be seen as a source of authority:

1. **JOB 19:25** – Job appears to refer to Jesus – "I know that my redeemer lives".

2. **ROMANS 2:14-16** – non-believers can have an innate sense for Christ, even if they do not recognise it – "They show that the requirements of the law are written on their hearts".

3. **MATTHEW 25:33-40** – the Parable of the Sheep and the Goats implies anyone living by altruistic love is working for Christ – whether they realise it or not. "What you do for the least person, you do for me" says Jesus.

HANS URS VON BALTHASAR – **CRITIC** of the '**ANONYMOUS CHRISTIAN**'. Multi-culturalism should not be an excuse to 'water down' the importance of Christ's crucifixion and resurrection.

Christian Teaching on Pluralism

PLURALISM is the view that there are many ways to salvation. Christianity is one of these. Human culture causes differences in beliefs and practices, but religions share the same ultimate goal.

KANT – there is a difference between the **NOUMENAL WORLD** (world as it really is) and the **PHENOMENAL WORLD** (world as it appears to us). Nature of God belongs to the noumenal world.

JOHN HICK – called for a **'COPERNICAN REVOLUTION'** in theology: to put God central – not Christianity. This call **AWAY FROM** a **CHRISTOCENTRIC** approach to theology is driven by our observations of the world, just as the **COSMOLOGICAL COPERNICAN REVOLUTION** was.

Religion is a **PHENOMENAL** attempt to understand God (by experience). All religions fall short of the truth. Christianity's 'truth claims' e.g. Virgin Birth, should be understood as myths expressing human relationship with 'the **REAL**'. God is **BENEVOLENT** and so salvation must be extended to all.

Hick's call for **DEMYTHOLOGIZATION** of the Bible has origins in **RUDOLF BULTMANN**. This is the idea that the Gospels do contain essential truths but these are revealed through **MYTHS**.

Hick argues it is impossible to create rational arguments for God e.g. **NATURAL THEOLOGY**. People are given reason to believe by **RELIGIOUS EXPERIENCES**. Knowledge of God is similar to our other knowledge of the world – through our experiences. Since individual experiences provide the grounding for belief, we must respect all religions, since none of them can provide universally-accepted argument for their beliefs. Experiences of God can be interpreted through the lens of different religions and faith is how we interpret these events. An **ANALOGY** is how different people respond differently to the same **MUSICAL STIMULUS**, influenced by their cultural background. Cultural influences might explain the differences in how people interpret the divine. Human projection shapes the experience but does not cause it.

Challenges to Pluralism

SUPPORTING HICK

- **FEUERBACH -** religious belief is projection. No genuine external cause of the religious experience

- **CUPITT -** challenges existence of God

- **PHILOSOPHICAL ARGUMENTS** – if 'the Real' is unknowable, we can't say anything meaningful about it and it cannot reveal itself deliberately to humans – this would make the revelation come from the human mind.

- Hick's theology allows for a **GLOBAL** theology and does not exclude polytheistic or non-theistic religions

OPPOSING HICK

- **INCARNATION** is regarded as central to Christianity, affirmed in the creed. Hick challenges traditional doctrines.

- **CHRISTIANS** might argue Hick undermines the essence of Christianity and reduces the Bible to fiction with morals.

- **LEE STROBEL** – 'the Case for Christ' – the gospels are eyewitness documents. But we know very little of Jesus' early life and the gospels were written after Jesus' death.

CONCLUSION OF HICK's PLURALISTIC HYPOTHESIS Empirical evidence, practical considerations and philosophical logic lend themselves to a Copernican revolution in theology.

How Was Hick Influenced by Kant?

The distinction between **NOUMENA** and **PHENOMENA** helps us to comprehend how different religions are talking about the same reality (noumena) but do so in different ways since our mind shapes our perception of our experiences (phenomena).

SYNOPTIC connection **PLATO** (Forms) -> **KANT** (noumena) -> **HICK**

RAIMON PANIKKAR – we need to be 'open' about the truth, rather than making claims about it. Life is a **'SEARCHING PILGRIMAGE'** and we might need to let go of traditions in order to find our identity. **CHRISTOPHANY** is God's way of making Himself known to people. **RELIGIOUS PLURALISM** is a **SPIRITUAL POSITION** not an intellectual position.

Issues Related to Pluralism and Christian Theology

CAN YOU BE 'MORALLY GOOD' AND YET NOT BE RELIGIOUS?

YES

- "8 He has shown you, O mortal, what is good.
  And what does the Lord require of you?
  To act justly and to love mercy
  and to walk humbly with your God." (Micah 6:8)

- "You see that a person is considered righteous by what they do and not by faith alone." (James 2:24)

- **SYNDERESIS** principle in **NATURAL LAW** suggests all human beings have the imprint of the law in their hearts. This orientates us towards good actions.

NO

- "Whoever believes in him is not condemned, but whoever does not believe stands condemned already because they have not believed in the name of God's one and only Son." (John 3:18)

- "For it is by grace you have been saved, through faith—and this is not from yourselves, it is the gift of God— 9 not by works, so that no one can boast." (Ephesians 2:8-9)

- "All have sinned and fall short of God's glory", (Romans 3:23)

WILL ALL GOOD PEOPLE BE SAVED?

NO

- James 2:14-24 – faith is incomplete without moral action. Salvation requires both and goodness alone is not enough.

- Faith saves, not deeds (**REFORMATION** core belief). Being good is irrelevant.The Reformation sees this as **JUSTIFICATION** by **WORKS**.

- Jesus Christ as 'the way' not 'a way' (John 14:6) - an **EXCLUSIVIST** claim

YES

- All are flawed as a result of 'the Fall' and so no one 'deserves' salvation

- Parable of the Sheep and Goats – judgment of God is based on **ACTION** not on faith. **ANONYMOUS CHRISTIANS** are those who live out the rule of love.

- God's **LOVE** will overrule **JUDGEMENT**

CAN THERE BE ANY OTHER MEANS OF SALVATION?

YES

- Revelation needs interpretation – including the narrative of Jesus' life

- There is no total agreement on what the 'truth' is and so faith is the result. Other religions also make claims through faith.

- Jesus is 'a truth' rather than 'the truth'.

- God's benevolence demands that He saves the good outside of Christianity too

NO

- **WILLIAM LANE CRAIG** – God's perfect knowledge' includes 'middle knowledge' of what people might have done if in different circumstances. God can therefore judge fairly.

- Jesus' life, death and resurrection are of **COSMIC** significance – a fulfilment of God's plan and so, is not just 'one of many' means of salvation.

- Pluralism undermines work of martyrs and missionaries. Missionary activity becomes irrelevant.

DOES THEOLOGICAL PLURALISM UNDERMINE CENTRAL CHRISTIAN BELIEFS?

YES

- Begs the question – which beliefs are central to Christianity and which are expressions of culture

- **HICK** proposed many mythological aspects – Virgin Birth, creation ex nihilo, doctrine of the Fall, Jesus' bodily resurrection – if so, what is left of Christianity?

- **PANIKKAR** undermines doctrine that there is no salvation outside of the church

NO

- **HICK** – doctrines are a phenomenal understanding of God

- **PANIKKAR** – emphasises God's revelation in Christ (**CHRISTOPHANY**) and does not suggest we reject Christian doctrines

CAN A LOVING GOD ULTIMATELY DENY ANY HUMAN BEING SALVATION?

YES

- A loving God would not force someone's choice – we must be free to choose to accept salvation (and accept consequences of not choosing)

- **AUGUSTINE** and **CALVIN** – God's love offers salvation to the elect (those predestined to be saved)

- A loving God would not extend salvation to the evil

- Christ's sacrifice would seem meaningless if salvation was offered to all

- Sheep and Goats (**MATTHEW 28**)– loving actions are a part of being offered salvation – not faith alone (**JUDGEMENT** on basis of actions)

NO

- **HICK** – God can freely make Himself known however He chooses. All can be saved and God judges out of love

- **BIBLE** suggests "it's not God's will that any should perish bit all should reach repentance" (even after death). (**2 PETER 3:9**)

Confusions to Avoid

1. Hick is NOT calling for one religion with everyone having the same beliefs – **GLOBAL THEOLOGY** is NOT the same as a **GLOBAL RELIGION**. He is emphasising that people necessarily have different ways of experiencing the divine.

2. Hick is NOT saying all religions are correct – rather, that they **CONTAIN TRUTH**. They also contain human projection and error and since we cannot know all truth, we must respect all religions.

3. For the belief system to be valid, it ought to lead people away from selfishness and towards ethical living. Therefore, not every belief system reflects the Divine.

Possible Exam Questions

1. "A theologically pluralist approach significantly undermines the central doctrines of Christianity." Discuss.

2. To what extent can non-Christians who live morally good lives and genuinely seek God be considered to be 'anonymous Christians'?

3. Critically assess the view that only Christianity offers the means of salvation

4. "Christianity is one of many ways to salvation." Discuss.

Key Quotes

1. "Those also can attain to salvation who through no fault of their own do not know the Gospel of Christ or His Church, yet sincerely seek God and moved by grace strive by their deeds to do His will as it is known to them through the dictates of conscience". (Catechism, paragraph 19)

2. "I know that my redeemer lives, and that in the end he will stand on the earth" Job 19:25

3. "All that matters (metaphysically) is that Jesus did rise from the dead, and that this act made salvation possible for all, irrespective of one's particular religion." (Religion, Key Concepts in Philosophy, 2007, p. 154)

4. "This is good, and pleases God our Saviour, who wants all people to be saved and to come to a knowledge of the truth". (1 Timothy 2:3-4)

5. "They show that the requirements of the law are written on their hearts". (Romans 2:14-16)

6. "Whoever believes in him is not condemned, but whoever does not believe stands condemned already because they have not believed in the name of God's one and only Son." (John 3:18)

7. "For it is by grace you have been saved, through faith—and this is not from

yourselves, it is the gift of God— [9] not by works, so that no one can boast." (Ephesians 2:8-9)

8. "You see that a person is considered righteous by what they do and not by faith alone." (James 2:24)

Suggested Reading

Hick's official website:
http://www.johnhick.org.uk/jsite/index.php/articles-by-john-hick

Philosopher Kings website:
http://www.philosopherkings.co.uk/hickandpluralism.html

Hick, J. (1995) God and the Universe of Faiths, SCM Press, Chapters 1 and 10

McGrath, A. (2010 5th Edition) A Christian Theology, Wiley-Blackwell, Chapter 17

D'Costa, G. (2009) Christianity and World Religions, Wiley-Blackwell

Religious Pluralism and Society

Background

In the 21st Century, a question that concerns many Christians is how they relate to people who follow no religion, or non-Christian beliefs. This goes together with the **MULTI-CULTURALISM** of Britain, leading it to become a multi-faith society. Issues arise for a Christian who might ask themselves whether to tolerate, or try to convert other people. Issues of religious expression in the workplace and attitudes towards sexuality have also made the public eye in the media. Christians might be unsure of how to voice their opinion without being discriminatory. Some Christians have become involved in **INTER-FAITH DIALOGUE**.

Specification

At A level, you will need to explain and evaluate:

1. The development of contemporary **MULTI-FAITH** societies – the reasons for this development, for example, migration

2. Christian responses to, including:

a. Responses of Christian communities to inter-faith dialogue

b. The scriptural reasoning movement (its methods and aims; and how the mutual study and interpretation of different religions' sacred literature can help understanding of different and conflicting religious truth claims)

3. How Christian communities have responded to the challenge of encounters with other faiths, for example:

a. Catholic Church: **REDEMPTORIS MISSIO** (**ENCYCLICAL**, pp. 55-57)

b. Church of England: Sharing the Gospel of Salvation (OCR A Level in Religious Studies Specification, 2016, p. 37)

Key Terms

ENCYCLICAL an open letter sent by the Catholic hierarchy to the churches, endorsed by the Pope

MISSIONARY WORK activity that aims to convert people to a particular faith or set of beliefs, or works for social justice in areas of poverty or deprivation

MULTI-FAITH SOCIETIES societies in which there are significant populations of people with different religious beliefs

SOCIAL COHESION when a group is united by bonds that help them to live together peacefully

SYNOD the legislative body of the Church of England

Structure of Thought - Pluralism and Society

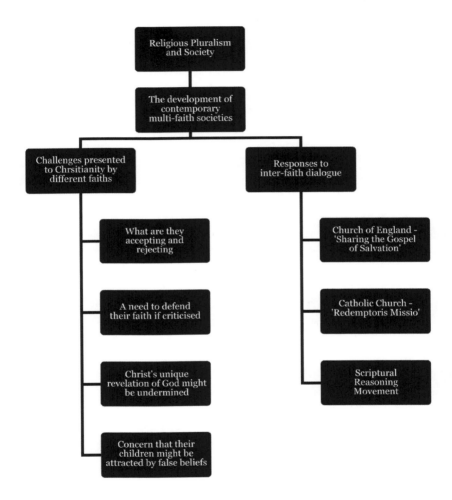

The Development of Multi-Faith Societies

EXAMPLE - MIGRATION

Christianity was introduced by the **ROMANS**. Before this, religious practices concentrated around worship of ancestors, fertility and agriculture. Christianity was established as the **PRIMARY FAITH** in Britain in **7th CENTURY**. Western development in **TRAVEL** and **COMMUNICATION** has increased **CULTURAL** and **RELIGIOUS DIVERSITY**. In the 1950s and 60s, the Textile industry was short of labour - encouraging immigration from **PAKISTAN** and the **CARIBBEAN**. **IDI AMIN** expelled the **ASIAN** population from **UGANDA** in 1972. This led to arrival in Britain of **HINDUS, MUSLIMS** and **SIKHS.**

People have travelled more for holiday and work and this has led to greater contact with different beliefs and traditions. 'Pockets' of religious groups were caused by religious people choosing to live near where others who practised the same religion. **SIKHS** arriving in 1950s for work tended to settle in **LONDON, BIRMINGHAM** and **WEST YORKSHIRE**; while the **JEWISH** population is higher in **NORTH LONDON** and **LEEDS**. When travelling, local etiquette needs respecting and for this, further education about beliefs is also needed.

MAX MULLER'S 19th century translations of Hindu texts into English (**THE SACRED BOOKS OF THE EAST**) increased interest in meditation and ideas such as **REINCARNATION**.

The changes have resulted in **MIXED-FAITH MARRIAGES,** the teaching of world faiths in schools, people working among **RELIGIOUS DIVERSITY**, the stocking of multi-faith **FESTIVAL FOODS** in supermarkets, **PRAYER ROOMS** in airports and hospitals, and an acceptance of **ATHEISM** and **AGNOSTICISM**, allowing religious beliefs to also be challenged.

Some argue that this new opportunity for the sharing of beliefs has helped to dispel prejudice and to **PROMOTE PEACE**. Others say it has helped **DEEPER REFLECTION** on one's own beliefs; while others still, claim tolerance is promoted at the expense of the **UNIQUE MESSAGE** of **SALVATION** through **CHRIST** promoted by the Christian mission.

Responses to Inter-faith Dialogue

Inter-faith dialogue is also known as inter-belief dialogue and inter-religious dialogue. It aims for mutual peace, respect, and cooperation. It aims to understand:

• Common ground and points of difference

• One's own faith while learning about, and from, beliefs of others

It is NOT about conversion but serves renewed interest in the wake of migration and human responses to tragedies such 9/11.

David Ford: The Future of Christian Theology

Inter-faith dialogue has new direction due to two major historical strands:

1. **HOLOCAUST**: the role played by Christianity in spurring on anti-Semitism

in contrast with those that opposed Nazism. **DABRU EMET** (**'SPEAK THE TRUTH'**) – was an invitation from Jewish leaders to Christians, calling for **CO-OPERATION**.

2. Rising **TENSIONS** between Islam and the West: **A COMMON WORD BETWEEN US AND YOU** – a call from Muslim leaders to Christianity outlining the responsibility of both to work for the common good of all.

Catholic Church - Redemptoris Missio (Mission of the Redeemer)

JOHN PAUL II – encouraged perseverance with the Christian mission in a multi-faith world. **PAPAL ENCYCLICALS** – letters from the Pope to Church leaders, are considered to be an authority and a 'final word.' **REDEMPTORIS MISSIO** (1990) re-visited the issues of **VATICAN II** and affirmed the essential place of Christian mission in a multi-faith world.

All religions provide spiritual opportunity, despite gaps and errors. The **LAITY** understand Christianity as lived through everyday life and so have a key role in dialogue.

All **CATHOLICS** have a duty to engage in **RESPECTFUL DIALOGUE**. This dialogue gives an opportunity to bear witness and is an 'expression' of Christian mission – not an opposition to it. The unique path to salvation through Christ is still offered by Christianity and should be emphasised.

Church of England - Sharing the Gospel of Salvation

1. 'THE DIALOGUE OF DAILY LIFE' – informal discussions of differing beliefs

2. 'THE DIALOGUE OF THE COMMON GOOD' – different faiths cooperate to help the community

3. 'THE DIALOGUE OF MUTUAL UNDERSTANDING' – formal debates e.g. Scriptural Reasoning

4. 'THE DIALOGUE OF SPIRITUAL LIFE' – meet for prayer and worship

This **FOURFOLD PLAN** to **SHARING THE GOSPEL OF SALVATION** is in response to **PAUL EDDY'S** 2006 question asking the Church to clarify the position of the Church of England on converting others. The plan affirmed that Jesus uniquely offers salvation and the Church of England has a mission to testify to this.

Christians should make efforts to speak about their beliefs openly and honestly but should not treat this as a 'marketing' exercise. Conversions are God's work – not the result of a 'good sell'.

Christians should make efforts to engage with members of different faiths – **MORE THAN JUST TOLERANCE.** Christians should follow the **GOLDEN RULE** – to 'treat others as you would like to be treated' (**LEVITICUS 19:18**) and should listen to others and leave judgement to God.

The Scriptural Reasoning Movement

How the mutual study and interpretation of different religions' sacred literature can help understanding of different and conflicting religious truth claims.

The movement began as a **JEWISH ACADEMIC FORUM** in the USA. In the mid-1990s, Christians asked to join to learn and found the conversations to be engaging. **MUSLIMS** were asked to join because of shared roots (**COMMON GROUND**) and together, the three religions can be known as **RELIGIONS OF THE BOOK** because each religion claims to have a holy text that is authoritative and revelatory. The movement now welcomes people of **ALL FAITHS**.

Cambridge Inter-faith Forum

This involves a discussion of themes considering scriptures of the Abrahamic faiths (those that come from a common origin in the **HEBREW** Scriptures) – Judaism, Christianity, Islam. Discussions are held in English in order to be inclusive. Discussions will concern earning, clothing, modesty, fasting, differing truth claims (e.g. Prophethood and Trinity) among other topics. The forum will consider how beliefs that appear similar are understood in their own contexts. Honesty and openness are encouraged.

Weaknesses

- Participants represent themselves – it is possible we lose sight of the normative teaching of each religion.

- It is difficult to decide if an interpretation is reasonable.

- It is questionable – the extent to which theological exclusivists can engage fully in inter-faith dialogue.

- Although open to all faiths, the extent to which non-Abrahamic faiths with varied origins and traditions can partake fully and benefit, is questionable.

- Some will criticise the relativizing of religious groups by treating all beliefs as equally valid.

Strengths

- Brings together people of different faiths, aiding tolerance in a multi-faith society.

- Collaboration socially and academically is encouraged.

- Face-to-face discussion is encouraged, as well as joint research. This further promotes inter-religious harmony and social cohesion through raised awareness and understanding of one's own views and those of others.

Issues

HAS INTER-FAITH DIALOGUE CONTRIBUTED PRACTICALLY TOWARDS SOCIAL COHESION?

YES

- Inter-faith groups have become more popular. Many societies and social events have come about as a result of increased dialogue.

- Inter-faith groups discuss points of difference and similarity; even if spiritual cohesion and not social cohesion is its aim.

- **SOCIAL COHESION** arguably requires mixing of schools and communities. **EDUCATIONAL REFORMS** such as **FREE SCHOOLS** encourage division and exclusivity.

NO

- Some disagree with inter-faith dialogue and believe that the mission should be to bring others to Christianity

- Many **CATHOLICS** disagreed with **VATICAN II'S** emphasis on inter-faith dialogue and so perhaps division within religions, rather than healing between faiths has been achieved

- Problems that divide society are not religious but are due to housing, social equality, income, and education.

- Religion is also becoming less important to people.

DOES SCRIPTURAL REASONING RELATIVISE RELIGIOUS BELIEFS?

YES

- Seems to dismiss idea that one religion holds the truth

- Encourages diversity of opinion and reasoning

- Does not tell people what to think; encourages a look within oneself, at experience, strengthening one's own faith

- Pluralists e.g. John Hick – relativisation could be a good thing, helping people accept no single religion can contain 'the truth'

- All responses to one reality, shaped by culture and tradition

NO

- Studying together implies each holy text has something to offer

- Karl **BARTH** – God is fully and **EXCLUSIVELY** revealed in Christ and the Bible – this should not be equally valid as other truth claims

- Exclusivists – Christians should focus on sharing their unique message and the dangers of not accepting this

SHOULD CHRISTIAN COMMUNITIES AIM TO CONVERT PEOPLE FROM OTHER FAITHS?

YES

- It is their duty to obey Christ's command to "go and make disciples of all nations" (**MATTHEW 28:19**)

- **REDEMPTORIS MISSIO** – Christians should make efforts to bring others to Christ: "Every person has the right to hear the 'Good News' of the God who reveals and gives himself in Christ" (para 23)

- New Testament emphasises the urgency and importance of Christian mission

NO

- An all-loving God would grant **UNIVERSAL** salvation

- **INCLUSIVISTS** would say salvation could be possible within other religious traditions as '**ANONYMOUS** Christians' (**RAHNER**)

- Religion is shaped by culture – there is no 'single ultimate truth'

- **PLURALISTS-** all religions are equally valid. Conversion is not necessary (Hick)

- Conversion might not be necessary if salvation is possible in one's own religious context

Confusions to Avoid

1. There is some debate as to whether conversion of those of no faith is significantly different to conversion of those of a previous faith. On the one hand, those converting from a previous faith might face bigger challenges because of their **FAMILY** and social group.

2. This tension might not be the same for someone of no religious background – thought, their social group might change. On the other hand, some **INCLUSIVISTS** might argue that the non-religious have a greater need to know God than the 'anonymous Christian' does. The non-religious might never have encountered the opportunity to become religious; while others might have actively opposed religion.

Possible Exam Questions

1. To what extent should Christians seek to convert others to Christianity at every opportunity?

2. "Inter-faith dialogue is of little practical use." Discuss.

3. To what extent does scriptural reasoning relativise religious beliefs?

4. "Converting people of no faith should be equally important to a Christian as converting people of non-Christian faith." Discuss.

Key Quotations

From Redemptoris Missio (paragraphs) and the Bible:

1. "Every person has the right to hear the 'Good News' of the God who reveals and gives himself in Christ" Para. 46

2. "In the light of the economy of salvation, the Church sees no conflict between proclaiming Christ and engaging in inter-faith dialogue" Para. 55

3. "The Church gladly acknowledges whatever is true and holy in the religious traditions of Buddhism, Hinduism and Islam as a reflection of that truth which enlightens all people" Para. 55

4. "Dialogue should be conducted and implemented with the conviction that the Church is the ordinary means of salvation and that she alone possesses the fullness of the means of salvation" Para. 55

5. "Dialogue leads to inner purification and conversion" Para. 56

6. "Inter-religious dialogue is a part of the church's evangelising mission" Para. 55

7. "Therefore go and make disciples of all nations, baptising them in the names of the Father and of the Son and of the Holy Spirit." (Matthew 28:19)

Suggested Reading

1. The Doctrine Commission of the Church of England (1995) The Mystery of Salvation Church House Publishing, Chapter 7

2. Ford, D. (2011) The Future of Christian Theology, Wiley-Blackwell, Chapter 7

3. Pope Paul VI (1965) Nostra Aetate; Declaration on the relation of the Church to non-Christian religions

The Challenge of Secularism

Background

The role of religion in Western Europe has changed and is changing. Christianity in Britain has been in decline — seen in Church attendance and solemnisation of fewer marriages. This reduction has led to questions from **PSYCHOLOGY** and **SOCIOLOGY** about the role of religious institutions in public life and culture. It has been suggested that religion should be seen as part of the '**PRIVATE**' rather than 'public' sphere while the relationship between Christianity and British culture is diminishing.

Specification

At A level, you will need to explain the rise of **SECULARISM** and **SECULARISATION**, and know and evaluate:

1. The views that God is an illusion and the result of wish fulfilment

2. The views of Freud and Dawkins that society would be happier without Christianity as it is infantile, repressive and causes conflict

3. The views that Christianity should play no part in public life

4. The views of **SECULAR HUMANISTS** that Christian belief is personal and should play no part in public life, including education and schools, and government and state (OCR A Level in Religious Studies Specification, 2016, p.

40). Be aware that there are two different approaches to secularism, and one of these argues that **SECULARISM** is absolutely necessary for religious toleration and diversity, (the other, argued by **DAWKINS**, argues that religion should be completely excluded form public life).

Key Terms

SECULAR not connected or associated with religious or spiritual matters

SECULARISM various meanings – a belief that religion should have no role in public or government life; a belief that no one religion should have a superior position in the state; a belief in a public space and a private space, and that religion should be kept apart from public power

SECULARISATION a theory rising out of Enlightenment thinking, developed in the 1950s and 1960s, that proposed that with the advancement of democracy and technology, religious belief would progressively decline. Such a linear decline is now doubted by sociologists

WISH FULFILMENT according to Freud, the satisfaction of a desire through a dream or other exercise of the imagination

Structure of Thought - Challenge of Secularism

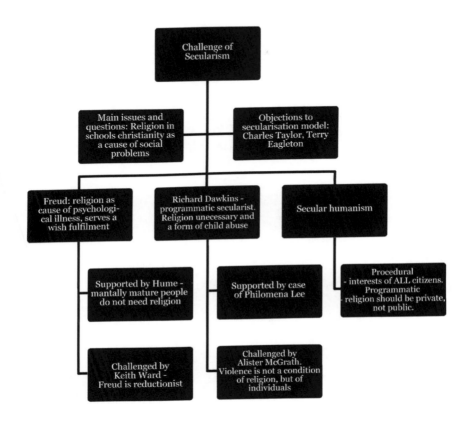

Challenge of Secularism

Main issues and questions: Religion in schools christianity as a cause of social problems

Objections to secularisation model: Charles Taylor, Terry Eagleton

Freud: religion as cause of psychological illness, serves a wish fulfilment

Richard Dawkins - programmatic secularist. Religion unecessary and a form of child abuse

Secular humanism

Supported by Hume - mantally mature people do not need religion

Supported by case of Philomena Lee

Procedural - interests of ALL citizens. Programmatic - religion should be private, not public.

Challenged by Keith Ward - Freud is reductionist

Challenged by Alister McGrath. Violence is not a condition of religion, but of individuals

The Rise of Secularism and Secularisation

Important Aims to Understand

1. Reasons for the rise of secularism and secularisation and the views that God is an illusion and the result of wish fulfilment

2. The views of Freud and Dawkins that society would be happier without Christianity as it is infantile, repressive and causes conflict

Difficulty in Defining Secularism

1. Measuring and defining terms: less Church attendance does not mean less spirituality

2. Influence and authority: new movements are being accepted by society, even with a decline in mainstream religions

3. Religious commitment and evidence of the past: Church attendance in previous years was not the best test of religious commitment. Today, people attend because they want to, not because they must. So, what really is an appropriate way of measuring secularisation?

AUGUSTE COMPTE - civilised society develops progressively from:

1. **Theological** perspective

2. **Metaphysical** (abstract) view of the world

3. **Positive** (scientific/rational) view of the world

Sigmund Freud

Religion is a key cause of **PSYCHOLOGICAL** illness. Tradition and conformity **REPRESS** natural instincts, and this leads to **NEUROSES**.

Freud considered that religion belongs to the **INFANTILE** – belief is formed in the early stage of human social development. This stage is before the person has developed the ability to reason and at this stage, needs external care and security provided by a **FATHER** and **MOTHER** figure (by **PROJECTION**, God and the Virgin Mary).

Supported by Hume

Mentally mature people do not need religion – it is practised by the uneducated.

Freud went further to say that religion was a **SICKNESS** and could be proven as such by his use of psychoanalysis.

When instinctual life wins and religion ends, humans will be content.

Wish Fulfilment

As children, there is a **VULNERABILITY** and helplessness that is fulfilled 'by a belief that injustices will be corrected, that life has a purpose, and that there is a moral code' (Freud, The Future of an Illusion). God – or belief in God – represents a **PERSONIFICATION** of our needs. Religion can answer questions that humans have that cannot be answered by studying 'what is real?'

Religion causes conflict as it creates unreliable and harmful answers to human uncertainty and matters outside of our control.

Challenges to Freud

KEITH WARD labels Freud a **REDUCTIONIST** because he appears to reduce everything to material terms. This is an **INADEQUATE** explanation for the spiritual experience of existence.

Truth claims about religion cannot be disproved.

Freud emphasises the **DESTRUCTIVE** nature of religion but for others, religion is an aide rather than a harm. It can assist understanding and acceptance of life. Religion can help to form communities rather than to divide them.

Freud **GENERALISES** religions – while some are hierarchical and controlling, not all are and therefore, not all religions can be seen to perpetuate guilt.

Wish fulfilment might not always lead to illusion – it can lead to creativity such as that seen in **DREAMS** and daydreams.

Richard Dawkins - Programmatic Secularism

In **THE GOD DELUSION**, Dawkins makes the case for:

1. Imagining a world without religion

2. Accepting that the God hypothesis is weak

3. Realising that religion is a form of child abuse

4. Accepting atheism with pride

Dawkins argued that life can be meaningful without reference to religion. The processes of nature can be most clearly explained by Charles Darwin and his **THEORY** of **EVOLUTION**.

Belief in God is **DELUDED** and unnecessary. Religion is delusional since it represents a persistent false belief going against the main body of evidence. The supernatural world cannot be subject to empirical study and therefore, Dawkins rejects **STEPHEN JAY GOULD'S** attempts to argue that religion and science are '**NON-OVERLAPPING MAGISTERIA**'. For Dawkins, ALL things must be able to be studies empirically.

RELIGION IS A FORM OF CHILD ABUSE – A child lacking understanding should not be labelled as religious. Dawkins criticised the state for allowing a child below the age of consent and reason to be labelled as religious. They have been unable to think about the beliefs they are labelled as possessing. This could be seen in school admissions, for example.

Dawkins used the example of **CATHOLICISM** as a form of long-term psychological abuse. He gave the example of Catholic women who had experienced sexual abuse, who found the fear of hell to be greater than the abuse itself. Another example was the '**HELL HOUSE**' thought of by a pastor in Colorado. Here, children were terrified by actors role-playing the sins of abortion and homosexuality, followed by the torture of Hell. Dawkins suggests that the power of belief in religion becomes greater than the physical abuse suffered.

EXAMPLE: PHILOMENA LEE

Had her child, born out of wedlock, taken from her by the Catholic Church. She stayed with her boy for three years at the Sean Ross Abbey in Roscrea – a place for unwed mothers. Philomena's boy was then sold, to be adopted by a Catholic family.

Responses to Dawkins - Alister McGrath

THE DAWKINS DELUSION

Many Christians think faith is not irrational. Furthermore, religion and science are not necessarily in conflict. Science can explain the intelligible universe and so **DAWKINS** is right to criticise the '**GOD OF THE GAPS**'. However, the intelligible universe could still point to an intelligent designer.

The relationship between science and religion can be **COMPLEMENTARY**, reflecting different aspects of human experience.

Dawkins' **LIMITED POSITIVIST VIEW** that metaphysical questions are outside of scientific enquiry and therefore meaningless is criticised by many scientists. Science, theology and philosophy can provide useful insights.

MCGRATH also criticised Dawkins' claim that violence was a necessary condition of religion. Jesus taught against violence – "turn the other cheek". Violence is a condition of certain individuals, not religion as a whole. McGrath also notes that atheism has also been a part of violence and repression, e.g. in communist regimes.

Secular Humanism - Christian Belief is Personal

Two Types of Secularism

1. **PROCEDURAL**: the interests of ALL citizens – religious and non-religious, should be considered by the state. Religion should be treated equally to other institutions but not with preference.

2. **PROGRAMMATIC**: in a **PLURAL** society, the state should be solely secular. This means religious views and practices should be kept apart from public institutions – schools, universities, public holiday and government.

The main aims of modern humanism were set out in the **AMSTERDAM DECLARATION** of 1952:

1. Humanism is **ETHICAL**: all humans are of worth, have dignity and autonomy

2. Humanism is **RATIONAL**: science should be used imaginatively and as a basis for solving human difficulties.

3. Humanism supports democracy and human **RIGHTS**: the best way in which humans can develop their potential.

4. Humanism insists that personal **LIBERTY** must be combined with **SOCIAL RESPONSIBILITY**: no dogmatic beliefs, the autonomous person has a responsibility to society and the natural world

5. Humanism is a response to the widespread demand for an alternative to dogmatic religion: continuous observation will build our reliable understanding of the world and revision of **SCIENTIFIC** understanding.

6. Humanism values artistic **CREATIVITY** and imagination: enhancing human existence. Novelist **E.M. FORSTER** defined the humanist as someone with "curiosity, a free mind, belief in good taste, and belief in the human race."

7. Humanism is a **LIFESTANCE** aiming at the maximum possible fulfilment: creative and ethical living can help us to achieve the challenges of the present

Education and Schools

GOVERNMENT AND STATE

1776 – Formation of the USA – Church and State made separate.

Keeping Church and State separate might be seen as one way of avoiding conflicting political aims between Christian denominations and even with other religions with the increase in migrants.

Alternative ideas about theocracy are seen in:

1. **DOMINIONISTS**: America should be ruled according to Biblical laws – based on Genesis 1:28 where humans are said to have dominion – this includes over the state. A view held mostly by Protestant, evangelical and conservative groups.

2. **RECONSTRUCTIONISTS**: Similar Dominionist notion. Seen in the Old Testament when the life of Israel was ordered according to laws given to Moses. Followed by Calvinists.

In England, the queen is the Head of the Church of England. 26 Bishops sit as **'LORDS SPIRITUAL'** in the **HOUSE OF LORDS**. Regardless of faith, church of England Parish Churches can be used for marriages, funerals and baptisms. This is a way of the state providing a spiritual life for everyone.

NOTE: England is NOT a **THEOCRACY.**

Some **PROGRAMMATIC SECULARISTS** believe the government should go further in separating Church and State.

ROWAN WILLIAMS – the Church has a role to play in resisting the apparent threat of secularism felt by some religious fundamentalists who are anti-democratic (as they oppose democratic consensus on laws such as legalisation of abortion and homosexuality reform)

CHRISTOPHER DAWSON – secular education systems bring challenges. They deprive people of the ability and right to make sense of their own culture

– a culture which, to a large extent, is immersed in religion.

Objections to the Secularisation Model

CHARLES TAYLOR – the '**SUBTRACTION STORIES**' of **DAWKINS** and **FREUD** show how the world can be explained with stories that show neither God, nor any 'greater being' is needed for us to live fulfilled lives.

This is '**SELF-SUFFICING HUMANISM**'. This humanism fails because it emphasises the individual and in so doing, loses the **COMMUNAL** aspect of society (notice though, a counter-argument, that humanists argue for **SOCIAL RESPONSIBILITY**). Rather than a discovery that God does not exist, our exclusion of God from our explanation of the world reflects a **WESTERN PHASE**. In order to live a full life, we need to embrace a sense of the divine and distance ourselves from secularism.

TERRY EAGLETON – A **MARXIST** and **CHRISTIAN** approach. Marxist in the sense that he thought it wrong to exclude religious imagination and its contribution to human existence. Eagleton thought the harm of religion should be weighed up against its positive contributions.

The **SPIRITUAL** aspect of human experience can be captured by religion, but not by secularism. People have been prepared to make ultimate sacrifices for truths about existence but not for **AESTHETIC** reasons e.g. sport/ music. Secularist privatisation has seemed to make religion and morality irrelevant. 9/11 showed the dangers of a **POSITIVIST** view of the world without religion where dangerous extremists interpret the Western secularists as trying to turn the world anti-religious.

Issues

IS CHRISTIANITY A MAJOR CAUSE OF PERSONAL AND SOCIAL PROBLEMS?

YES

- Patriarchal and sexist

- Definition of women in terms of motherhood and exaltation of virginity (Virgin Mary)

- Role played in criminalisation of homosexuality

- Dawkins – "American Taliban" – evangelical Christians who say AIDS is God's punishment to homosexuals

- Dawkins – an absolutist faith cannot comprehend belief systems outside of their own and so try to influence the law to criminalise things that differ to their own moral law

- Sanctity of life – dangerous. Irony of George Bush overseeing state executions while still preventing research on embryonic life

NO

- The reverse can be said to be true – e.g. religious leaders who led social change eg William **WILBERFORCE** (anti-slavery) OR **ARCHBISHOP**

WILLIAM TEMPLE

- 19th century – Christian churches established schools for the poor in England. **LORD SHAFTESBURY** establishes **RAGGED SCHOOLS** for the poor.

- Decriminalisation of homosexuality in the 1960s was supported by Anglican Bishops at a time that people resisted change

- Religious challenge to segregation e.g. Martin Luther King Jr

- Food banks

ARE SECULARISM AND SECULARISATION OPPORTUNITIES FOR CHRISTIANITY TO DEVELOP NEW WAYS OF THINKING AND ACTING?

YES

- **DAVID FORD (THE FUTURE OF CHRISTIAN THEOLOGY)** – The beginning of secularism led to the idea of state tolerance. The idea of public good is not threatened by religious conflict.

- **KWAME APPIAH (MISTAKEN IDENTITIES: CREED, COUNTRY, COLOUR)** – Religion can change in response to the society it meets. This change can be fast or slow. Change in behaviour or practice can lead to a change in beliefs. Appiah draws attention to how scripture is interpreted and sometimes discarded if it is unable to adapt to society – examples include Babylonian babies being killed and First Peter's references to the submission of slaves.

- **PETER BERGER (THE DESECULARISATION OF THE WORLD)** – Claims that secularisation theory is mistaken in saying religious institutions are not adapting to a secular world. Instead, he claims, religious institutions are surviving and sometimes flourishing.

- Some would say secularism and secularisation are good opportunities for Christianity to **DEVELOP** its ways of engaging with present-day issues e.g. of genetic engineering, sexuality and the changing roles of men and women.

NO - Development nothing to do with Secularism

- **DAVID MARTIN (THE EVANGELICAL UPSURGE AND ITS POLITICAL IMPLICATIONS)** – Doubts the decline in religion predicted by secularisation theory. The 1980s onwards has seen a global increase in conservative Christianity and Islam.

- However, although Christianity is the largest religion in Britain, it is outnumbered by people of **NO RELIGION** (2015 survey - 51%). This brings into question the extent to which Christianity should remain a significant contributor to society's culture and values. One example is whether Christianity should be prioritised as subject of study in Religious Education.

- Others might say these changing ways of thinking are already reflected in the number of **DENOMINATIONS** within Christianity. These reflect changing thoughts – with some allowing divorce, women Priests and some not even having clergy.

- The question remains as to whether religion informs society or whether society informs religious evolution. Christianity **CONTRIBUTES** significantly to the culture and values of society e.g. the State holidays follow Christian festivals and the remembrance services include prayers and hymns., yet **ETHICAL AGENDA** often driven by secularism and emphasis on **HUMAN RIGHTS**.

THE QUESTION OF FAITH SCHOOLS

YES - A Good Thing

- Faith schools reflect the **DIVERSITY** of Britain.

- The **VALUES** (spiritual and moral) that form a foundation of faith school education, enhance the wider curriculum rather than detract from it.

- Faith schools support social **COHESION** as they value local religious groups.

- Faith schools offer a popular **CHOICE** for parents.

- Faith schools have a better understanding of faith than non-religious schools and not every faith school has religious belief as an entrance requirement.

- Faith schools can offer support for **BOTH** religious and non-religious beliefs.

NO - A Bad Thing

- Pupils fail to be **INTEGRATED** into wider society – communities are isolated

- Teaching of science is questionable e.g. evolution as one theory alongside others such as **CREATIONISM**

- Pupils left open to **RADICALISATION**

- Faith development should be facilitated by the community as it is a **PRIVATE** matter – it should not be any responsibility of the state

- Religious education should be part of a broad curriculum teaching a **SPECTRUM** of belief and making the point that some religious claims e.g. Golden rule, are no different to non-religious truth claims.

Key Confusions to Avoid

1. The discussion concerning whether spiritual values are just 'human values' can sometimes lead to confusion. To say spiritual values are just 'human', implies that there is no 'significant other' to which they are directed or from which they come.

2. Arguments to support this include the belief that values often labelled as 'Christian' are actually fundamental values of being human and part of flourishing in society. Such values include those of **COMPASSION, FORGIVENESS, JUSTICE, AND PEACE**. Furthermore, those who argue that these spiritual values are no different to 'being human', might add that the aforementioned values do not require a belief in God or an afterlife in order to be endorsed.

3. On the other hand, there are arguments that spiritual values are much more than simply 'human'. For example, some spiritual values such as self-

sacrifice and 'love your enemies' do not always benefit the human. Spiritual values are untainted by human, material desires, and express a commitment to something 'other'. Furthermore, it has been suggested that the **UNIVERSAL DECLARATION OF HUMAN RIGHTS** is based on the belief that humans have 'ultimate worth'. This could support the idea that human values are 'spiritual', rather than the other way round'.

4. Lastly, there is an argument that human and spiritual values cannot be made separate and this was shown in the **INCARNATION**.

Possible Exam Questions

1. "Christianity has a negative impact on society." Discuss.

2. To what extent are Christian values more than just basic human values?

3. "Christianity should play no part in public life." Discuss.

4. Critically assess the claims that God is an illusion and the result of wish fulfilment.

Key Quotes

1. "Faith is the root of freedom and programmatic secularism cannot deliver anything comparable". Rowan Williams, Faith in the Public Square, 2012, page 32

2. "9/11 highlights two extremes of anxiety: faithless Western secular

atheism and its fear of religion (and hence its reaction as the 'war on terror') and faithful religious fundamentalism and its fear of positivism, capitalism and secularisation". Michael Wilcockson, Religious studies for A Level Year 2, 2017, page 277

3. "No, our science is no illusion. But an illusion it would be to suppose that what science cannot give us we can get elsewhere". Sigmund Freud, The Future of an Illusion, 2001, page 56

4. "The presence or absence of a creative super-intelligence is unequivocally a scientific question". Richard Dawkins, The God Delusion, 2006, page 59

5. "Dawkins' naïve view that atheists would never carry out crimes in the names of atheism simply founders on the cruel rocks of reality". Alister McGrath and Joanna Collicutt McGrath, The Dawkins Delusion?, 2007, page 78

6. "There is something infantile in the presumption that somebody else (parents in the case of children, God in the case of adults) has a responsibility to give your life meaning and point." Richard Dawkins, The God Delusion, 2006, p. 404

7. "The religions of mankind must be classed as among the mass delusions". Sigmund Freud, Civilisation and its Discontents, 1930, page 81

8. "Children, I'll argue, have a human right not to have their minds crippled by exposure to other people's bad ideas". Nicholas Humphrey, 'What Shall We Tell the Children?' Amnesty Lecture, 21 February 1997,

Suggested Reading

1. British Humanist Society, https://humanism.org.uk/

2. Dawkins, R. The God Delusion, Chapter 9

3. Dawson, C. (1956) 'The Challenge of Secularism' in Catholic World, also online: http://www.catholiceducation.org/en/education/catholic-contributions/the-challenge-of-secularism.html

4. Ford, D. (2011) The Future of Christian Theology, Wiley-Blackwell, Chapters 3 and 6

5. Freud, S. The Future of an Illusion

Liberation Theology and Marx

Background

Marx introduced the idea that when humans are unable to live fulfilling lives due to being 'dehumanised', this results in a form of **ALIENATION**. Humans are **DEHUMANISED** when they are **EXPLOITED,** and this is a result of being treated as objects and used as a means to an end.

Marx's teachings on alienation and exploitation have been used by **LIBERATION THEOLOGY** to analyse the '**STRUCTURAL'** causes of **SOCIAL SIN** that have led to poverty, violence, and injustice. Such 'structural' causes include capitalism and institutions (schools, churches, and the state).

The analysis of structural sin has led to a call for the **'PREFERENTIAL OPTION FOR THE POOR'** – a thought calling for Christians to act in solidarity with the poor, rooted in the Gospel. The implication of this teaching is to place **ORTHOPRAXIS** (right action) before **ORTHODOXY** (official Church teaching).

Specification

At A Level, you will need to explain and evaluate the relationship of liberation theology and Marx, including:

1. Marx's teaching on **ALIENATION** and exploitation

2. **LIBERATION THEOLOGY**'s use of Marx to analyse social sin

3. Liberation theology's teaching on the '**PREFERENTIAL OPTION** for the poor'

Key Terms

ALIENATION: The process of becoming detached or isolated

BASIC CHRISTIAN COMMUNITIES: Christian groups that gather to try to directly resolve problems in their lives

CAPITALISM: An economic system in which the means of production are privately owned and operated for profit, in contrast with communism where the state controls trade and industry

ORTHODOXY: Right belief

ORTHOPRAXIS: Right action

PREFERENTIAL OPTION FOR THE POOR: Acting in solidarity with the poor and oppressed

STRUCTURAL SIN: Social dimension of sin, beyond individual sin. It is an attitude of society that contributes to oppression

Structure of Thought - Liberation Theology and Marx

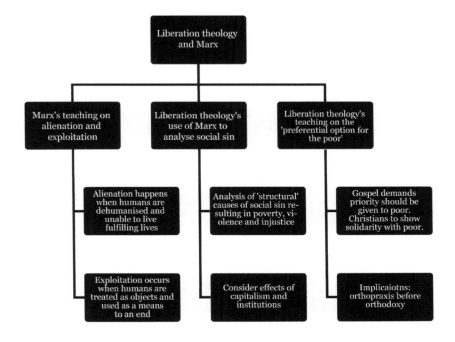

Marx's Teaching on Alienation and Exploitation

Marx taught that alienation occurs when humans are dehumanised and unable to live fulfilling lives. **EXPLOITATION** occurs when humans are treated as objects and used as a means to an end. Note the similarity to Kant's second formulation of the **CATEGORICAL IMPERATIVE** here (treat people not just as a means to an end but always also as an **END** in themselves).

For example, consider a recent purchase from someone you might not know. You might have bought a sandwich from a local supermarket. Did you stop to think about the person serving you at the till? Or, in today's times of 'self-service' – have you thought of the people involved in the building and maintenance of the machines, the famers producing the ingredients needed for the bread and filling of your purchase?

Marx's teaching on **ALIENATION** and exploitation help us to think about the people involved in the **PRODUCTION** of things we value. Marx would say it does matter and should matter that we appreciate the persons involved in the stages of production and do not just see them as a means of production. If we do the latter, we alienate them from society.

Furthermore, technology has revolutionised the world but with the more apparent power we have in this development, the less in control we actually feel. Marx said there is a **HUMAN CAUSE** behind this feeling of powerlessness.

When humans reached the ability to produce **SURPLUS TO REQUIREMENTS**, the favour was granted to those who controlled the means of production and herein beginS class division. This division is evident through the ownership of land, where labour is bought and sold – people are treated as means and not 'ends'. Marx laid the foundations for **SOCIALISM** and **COMMUNISM** through his criticism of **CAPITALISM** – the private ownership of land. This private ownership changed the relationship between people and the means of production, leading to the exploitation and alienation of the workers.

What does this look like?

1. FEUDAL LORDS own the land and the means of producing food.

2. SERFS work on the land but don't own it. They rely on feudal lords for access and must give surplus to feudal lords.

3. SUBSERVIENT Serfs alienated from the land on which they work.

This system can be likened to working in a factory. Here, people only understand the part they work on and do not have sight of the whole process. In this way, they are **DEHUMANISED**. The work is necessary as without it, we could not pay for our survival. In this way, exploitation becomes a means to an end. Workers form part of a supply chain and do not know the 'purchasers'.

Neither do those purchasing know the workers - people are **ALIENATED** from their work. Our 'happiness' at cheap prices comes at the expense of other people's happiness - at the expense of the exploitation of others.

Liberation Theology's Use of Marx and Social Sin

Liberation theology began as an **INTELLECTUAL** and **PRACTICAL THEOLOGICAL** movement among those who worked with the poor.

PAULO FREIRE described the process of **'CONSCIENTISATION'** – a process by which someone becomes aware of the power structures in society. **FREIRE** argued that education should teach people to read the power structures and should work to **TRANSFORM** society and not to just transmit information.

Traditionally, theology had focussed on passing on information. **LIBERATION THEOLOGY** focused on **ACTION** before **EXPLANATION** – **ORTHOPRAXY** before **ORTHODOXY**. Liberation theology became, therefore, a **THEOLOGY OF ACTION**.

Liberation theology proposed that the **KINGDOM OF GOD** is not a place we go to when we die; but is something to work for in this life.

GUSTAVO GUTIÉRREZ, one of the founders of liberation theology, proposed that liberation occurs two-fold:

1. SOCIAL AND ECONOMIC – poverty and oppression are the consequence of human choices and therefore humans can resolve as well. Hence an idea of **SOCIAL SIN**.

2. FROM SIN – to be reconciled with the Divine.

Both 'social and economic' and 'from sin' aspects of liberation must happen together. Gutiérrez claimed that **POLITICAL LIBERATION** is the work of salvation. He emphasised earthly liberation, whereas **JUAN SEGUNDO** emphasised spiritual liberation.

The Bible extracts in the 'key quotations' section allow you to consider how each teaching might have influenced the development of liberation theology. For example, **MATTHEW 25:40** - "whatever you did for one of the least of these brothers and sisters of mine, you did for me" – encourages the **PREFERENTIAL OPTION FOR THE POOR** in the call to side with **'ONE OF THE LEAST'**, i.e. an outcast.

Liberation theology has its origins in 1960s Latin America, a place of corrupt governments and poverty. Christian groups formed to discuss experiences and practical solutions. Liberation theology therefore became a **THEOLOGY OF HOPE**, with God's love extending both to creation and to liberation.

LATIN AMERICA had found itself at a crossroads, a significant battleground in the cold war conflict between the USA and USSR. Marx had predicted a violent uprising of the oppressed – this seemed to be happening. Liberation theology focused on increasing **HUMAN WELL-BEING** rather than **HUMAN MATERIAL WEALTH**. This links to Marx's understanding that industrialisation can sacrifice the well-being of humans, despite the increase in wealth.

Liberation theology's use of Marx here, seems to be that the process of industrialisation is supported by a structure of sin that then forms part of the organisation of society, and in turn, part of the systems of government and education.

GUTIÉRREZ warned against using every aspect of Marxism but mentions his theories of alienation and exploitation. Gutiérrez also utilises Marx's suggestion that human beings can change the world they inhabit. Gutiérrez considered that people of Latin America wanted to be liberated from capitalism and so he called for the Church to stand with such movements for liberation – **BEING CHRISTIAN NECESSITATES BEING POLITICAL**. Gutiérrez went as far as to say that to not get involved in politics would be equal to helping to keep things the same, even if this situation was wrong/undesirable.

The **STRUCTURAL SIN** that must be changed can be seen in the injustices experienced by the oppressed. The current social system is one of structural inequality. By failing to address the class struggle, we legitimise the existing system, and in so doing, we act as a part of it. Perhaps Marx's most important contribution to liberation theology is his emphasis on recognising the class struggle against the structures of sin.

Liberation Theology's Teaching on "Preferential Option for the Poor'

The **GOSPEL** demands that Christians must give priority to the poor and act in **SOLIDARITY** with them. Liberation theology demands we put **ORTHOPRAXIS** before **ORTHODOXY**.

The teaching on **PREFERENTIAL OPTION FOR THE POOR** refers to a **BIBLICAL TREND** to show favour to the oppressed and outcasts. This follows the example set by Jesus – "whatever you did for one of the least of these brothers and sisters of mine, you did for me" **(MATTHEW 25:40).** The phrase was first coined by **FATHER ARRUPE, SUPERIOR GENERAL OF THE JESUITS** in **1968**, and was later picked up by the Catholic bishops of **LATIN AMERICA**. **JUAN SEGUNDO** taught that a preferential option for the poor shows an **AUTHENTIC CHRISTIAN RESPONSE**, avoiding the dangers of neutrality.

JUAN SEGUNDO wrote that the Church "intends to struggle, by her own means, for the defence and advancement of the rights of mankind, especially of the poor". Since we are made in **GOD'S LIKENESS, HUMAN DIGNITY** should be central to what we do. By failing to intervene and by allowing an ongoing social divide, we would prove incompatible with the peace and justice advocated in the Bible.

SEGUNDO differed to **GUTIÉRREZ** because he argued that liberation from sin **(SPIRITUAL LIBERATION)** should come before **SOCIAL LIBERATION**. This is because he felt social liberation might not be possible. After all, even Jesus taught that "the poor you will always have with you, but you will not always have me" (Matthew 26:11). Despite this, Segundo still taught that we should prioritise the poor and the preferential option for the poor has now gained acceptance beyond liberation theology.

JOHN PAUL II used the term in his encyclical **CENTESIMUS ANNUS** (1991). In this, he argued that support of the poor is an opportunity for the moral and cultural growth of humankind. However, this also includes a care for **SPIRITUAL POVERTY** – not just a focus on material wealth:

"This option is not limited to material poverty, since it is well known that there are many other forms of poverty, especially in modern society – not only economic but cultural and spiritual poverty as well". (Centesimus Annus para 43)

This spiritual poverty can be caused by focusing too much on the material goods. **POPE PAUL II** referenced drug and pornography addiction as an indication of a broken social structure. A destructive reading of human needs leaves a spiritual void that is filled by exploitation of the weak. **POPE FRANCIS** encourages the Catholic Church to be a **'POOR CHURCH FOR THE POOR'**.

The **CATHOLIC CHURCH** was concerned about the theological use of Marx as some of Marx's ideas were considered intolerable and thus a danger to use in theology **(CARDINAL RATZINGER).** Furthermore, Ratzinger (later Pope Benedict XVI) also claimed that using Marx interfered with the **EUCHARISTIC CELEBRATION** of power struggle. Evangelism was in danger of being superseded by violent revolution. Christian liberation should focus on **LIBERATION FROM SIN**, with God being the ultimate liberator. Marxism, Ratzinger claimed, was inherently un-Christian.

BONAVENTURE (1221-74), in **TEMPTATIONS FOR THE THEOLOGY OF LIBERATION (1974)**, criticised liberation theology for prioritising action over the Gospel. He claimed that liberation theology equated theology with politics, and as a result, side-lined Christian evangelism. Bonaventure highlighted that liberation theology focused on structural and not personal sin – despite Jesus' emphasis on **PERSONAL RECONCILIATION** with God.

However, for the starving and oppressed, one can question whether liberation from sin is more important than social liberation. Jesus did teach the importance of inner spiritual change, but he also called for real action – seen in the **PARABLE OF THE SHEEP AND THE GOATS (MATTHEW 25)**. The election of a Latin American Pope might signal the beginning of real impact of liberation theology. Pope Francis named **OSCAR ROMERO** a martyr and asked Gutiérrez to be a keynote speaker at a Vatican event in 2015.

However, in a 2017 visit to **MYANMAR** Pope Francis failed to explicitly denounce the persecution of the **ROHINGYA** Muslims by supposedly pacifist Buddhists.

Key Issues

SHOULD CHRISTIAN THEOLOGY ENGAGE WITH ATHEIST SECULAR IDEOLOGIES?

YES

- **ALASTAIR KEE** – liberation theology should make **MORE** use of Marx's premise that every historical stage demands a re-assessment of beliefs and ideas – including those of religion- liberation theology has been too conservative.

- Christian theology engages well with new ideas e.g. re-evaluation of **CREATIONISM** considering science

- To engage with all aspects of life, Christianity must engage with **SECULAR** thought as increasing numbers of people do not believe

NO

- **CARDINAL RATZINGER** – warns of liberation theology's dangerous and 'insufficiently critical' use of Marxist concepts

- Be wary of **UNDERMINING DISTINCTIVENESS** of Christianity - bigger than a **POLITICAL** movement

- Inspiration should come from Gospel – Marxist principles should never be central (**LEONARDO BOFF**)

DOES CHRISTIANITY TACKLE SOCIAL ISSUES MORE EFFECTIVELY THAN MARXISM?

YES

- Communism fails to respond effectively to poverty e.g. could not hold back **GLOBALISATION** (China and Cuba opening to capitalism)

- Christianity can be seen to be of more practical help as it focuses on well-being of **WHOLE** individual (spiritual and physical)

- Christianity provides hope and solace (salvation) for those who suffer, unlike Marxism.

- Charitable acts being a manifestation of the **KINGDOM** of God

NO

- Marx argued revolution would bring about a **CLASSLESS** society

- Marx might be seen to provide more practical advice for those without a belief in the Divine

- Marx argued Christianity an "opiate of the masses', drugging people into accepting a **FALSE CONSCIOUSNESS** (acceptance of an unjust situation) - link with **FREUD** and Future of an Illusion (**SECULARISM**)

- Christianity can get lost in **ORTHODOXY** before **ORTHOPRAXIS**

HAS LIBERATION THEOLOGY ENGAGED WITH MARXISM FULLY ENOUGH?

YES

- To promote social change but not at expense of Gospel

- Uses Marxism as a way of looking at poverty and thinking about ways of overcoming it

NO

- Fails to fully appreciate Marx's principle belief in the need for **REVOLUTION** (despite some liberation theology Priests taking off their dog collars and taking up arms in S. American struggles of 60s and 70s)

- **JOSÉ MIRANDA** – Marxism is more relevant today and greater dialogue is needed. Both Marxism and Christianity emphasise history and both speak of an approaching event that will bring about significant change

- **DENYS TURNER** – liberation theology should engage further with Marxism using the **APOPHATIC WAY** - **VIA NEGATIVA** (speaks only in terms of what may **NOT** be said about the perfect goodness that is God). For theology to have meaningful dialogue with Marxism, it needs to be based on a God that is ineffable.

IS IT RIGHT FOR CHRISTIANITY TO PRIORITISE ONE GROUP OVER ANOTHER?

YES

- Should favour the poor - part of **ISAIAH**'s call to **JUSTICE** (Isaiah 60)

- Following example of Jesus - redistribution in **FEEDING** of the **5000**

- **BOFF AND BOFF** – God takes sides with the poor – "Out of love, God takes sides, takes their side against the repressive measure of all pharaohs"

- Liberation theology suggests God takes sides

- God is the ultimate liberator, "the oppressed go free".

- **JOHN PAUL II** – wealth does not protect people from spiritual poverty

Spiritual poverty is also a focus in the Bible – "Blessed are the poor in spirit" (Matthew 5:3)

NO

- Jesus' message of salvation is for all humankind

- Poverty encompasses both spiritual and material

- **JUSTIFICATION** by faith, not by works - personal salvation is the key not social reform

Confusions to Avoid

Liberation theology would claim it is not Marxist, but rather, makes use of Marx's analysis of society. Within liberation theology, Marxism is not treated on its own – it is always considered in relation to the situation of the poor. Marxism is of '**INSTRUMENTAL**' use to liberation theology – an instrument in understanding and responding to the needs of the oppressed. For more on this, read **BOFF** in 'recommended reading'.

Christianity would claim that its 'preferential option for the poor' came from the Bible and that Marx's criticism of religion was based on corruptions in which the Church had contributed to oppression.

Liberation theology's call for **ORTHOPRAXIS** (living) before orthodoxy (dogma) might imply that the church had not advocated Christian action. This is not true. Christianity had always advocated putting beliefs into practice (see **JAMES** "faith without works is dead'). Liberation theology brought to attention the need of religion to affect the whole life – including an active role in the traditionally more secular areas of politics and **ECONOMICS**. This is what made liberation theology distinctive.

Possible Exam Questions

1. To what extent should Christianity engage with atheist secular ideologies?

2. "Liberation theology has not engaged with Marxism fully enough." Discuss.

3. Critically assess the claim that Christianity has tackled social issues more effectively than Marxism.

4. Critically assess the relationship of liberation theology and Marx with particular reference to liberation theology use of Marx to analyse social sin.

Quotations

1. "The growth of the Kingdom is a process which occurs historically in liberation". (Gutiérrez, A Theology of Liberation, 1973, p. 177)

2. "Then the Lord said to Moses, "Go to Pharaoh and say to him, 'This is what the Lord, the God of the Hebrews, says: "Let my people go, so that they may worship me." (Exodus 9:1).

3. He has performed mighty deeds with his arm; he has scattered those who are proud in their inmost thoughts. He has brought down rulers from their thrones but has lifted up the humble. He has filled the hungry with good things but has sent the rich away empty. (Luke 1:51-53)

4. "Again I tell you, it is easier for a camel to go through the eye of a needle than for someone who is rich to enter the kingdom of God." (Matthew 19:24).

5. "The King will reply, 'Truly I tell you, whatever you did for one of the least of these brothers and sisters of mine, you did for me.' (Matthew 25:40).

6. "For my Father's will is that everyone who looks to the Son and believes in him shall have eternal life, and I will raise them up at the last day." (John 6:40).

7. "Blessed are the poor in spirit, for theirs is the kingdom of heaven. (Matthew 5:3).

8. Social division whereby the worker "is depressed...both intellectually and physically, to the level of a machine" (Karl Marx, Early Writings, [1833-4] 1975, p.285

9. "Education is part of the machine of capitalism and pupils are the cogs in that machine" Libby Ahluwalia and Robert Bowie, Oxford A Level Religious Studies for OCR Year 2, 2017, page 305.

10. "In Latin America to be Church today means to take a clear position regarding both the present state of social injustice and the revolutionary process which is attempting to abolish that injustice and build a more human order." Gustavo Gutiérrez, A Theology of Liberation, 1974, p. 265;

11. "It is a will to build a socialist society, more just, more free, and human, and not a society of superficial and false reconciliation and equality." Gustavo Gutiérrez, A Theology of Liberation, 1974, p. 273-412.

12. "Liberation theology used Marxism purely as an instrument. It does not venerate it as it venerates the gospel". Leonardo Boff and Clodovis Boff,

Introducing Liberation Theology, 1987

13. "Let us recall the fact that atheism and the denial of the human person, his liberty and rights, are at the core of the Marxist theory". Congregation of the Doctrine of the Faith, Instruction on Certain Aspects of the 'Theology of Liberation', 1984, para 7.6

Suggested Reading

Boff, L. and Boff, C. (1987) Introducing Liberation Theology, Burnes and Oates

Gutierrez, G. (1974/2000) A Theology of Liberation, SCM Press, Chapter 4

Congregation of the Doctrine of the Faith (1984) Instruction on certain Aspects of the 'Theology of Liberation'

Wilcockson, M. (2011) Christian Theology, Hodder Education, Chapter 7

Influence of Marx – online resource.
See http://www.philosopherkings.co.uk/Marx.html

Gender and Society

Background

The Christian Church has lagged behind changes in social attitudes (and UK laws) in recent years, particularly on sexual issues such as **CONTRACEPTION**, **ABORTION** and **PRE-MARITAL SEX**, and gender issues such as attitudes to **HOMOSEXUALITY** (including gay marriage). For example, the Church of England still formally disallows homosexual gay partnerships in the **CLERGY** whilst professing to welcome gay church members. Gender issues also include attitudes to **TRANSEXUALS** and the political implications of **FEMINISM**.

Key Terms

ESSENTIALIST THEORIES: Gender is fixed by objective human nature, either by God or by our inherent biology (eg genes)

EXISTENTIALIST THEORIES: Gender is determined by social discourse (Foucault), by upbringing (Freud), or by social conditioning (including religious conditioning)

FEMINISM: A movement and a philosophy emerging form the Enlightenment emphasis on equal rights, but embracing theories of power and social conditioning.

SEX: Refers to the biological and physiological characteristics that define men and women

GENDER: The state of being classified as male or female or transgender (typically used with reference to social and cultural differences rather than biological ones).

FALSE CONSCIOUSNESS: Beliefs and behaviour induced by social attitudes and values which contradict the true interest (economic, political or social) of a person

PATRIARCHY: A system of society or government in which men hold the power and women are largely excluded from it.

ETERNAL FEMININE: Simone de Beauvoir's term to describe the role of woman as some ideal imposed by men (submissive housewife, sex object etc).

Specification

A Level requires us to study the effects of changing views of **GENDER** and gender roles on Christian thought and practice, including:

• Christian teaching on the roles of men and women in the family and society

• Christian responses to contemporary **SECULAR** views about the roles of men and women in the family and society including reference to:

 - Ephesians 5:22–33

 - Mulieris Dignitatem 18–19

The ways in which Christians have **ADAPTED** and **CHALLENGED** changing attitudes to family and gender, including issues of:

- motherhood/parenthood

- different types of family (single parent, extended, nuclear etc)

Note: there is not one, but **MANY** Christianities. The specification mentions just one Bible passage of many that need to be taken, and one Roman Catholic Document, Mulieris Dignitatem, in the context of a history of **PAPAL ENCYCLICALS**. Roman Catholics and Evangelical Christians argue against women leadership for different reasons. Quakers have always espoused strict equality.

Gender – Essentialist or Existentialist

ESSENTIALIST gender is essential to biology eg Biblical account of creation "God created them male and female'. Often includes conclusions about roles and/or intelligence eg men are stronger and wiser (**AQUINAS**).

EXISTENTIALIST gender is a product of **CIVILISATION** (de Beauvoir), male expectation, a cultural interpretation of gender roles, or an interpretation of the Bible. E.g. body image is a cultural construction (modern anorexic images very different from Rubens portraits).

Exploitation and Power (Michael Foucault)

The idea that human beings have a **SEXUALITY** is a recent western social phenomenon.

At the start of the 18th century, there was an emergence of "a political, economic, and technical incitement to talk about sex,"with experts speaking about the morality and rationality of sex, fuelled by Catholic teaching on sex, sin and confession" (Foucault).

ENLIGHTENMENT emphasises the empirical nature of sex and gender eg biological differences between men and women, the nature and source of sexual pleasure and supposed **OBJECTIVE** measures of intelligence and emotion

The "world of perversion" that includes the sexuality of children, the mentally ill, and homosexuality all subject to more vigorous prosecution. The labelling of **PERVERSION** conveyed a sense of "pleasure and power" for academics studying sexuality and the 'perverts' themselves.

HYPOCRISY as Middle Class society exhibited "blatant and fragmented perversion," readily engaging in perversion but regulating where it could take place. In 18th century Britain 1 in 5 women were prostitutes – Nelson's mistress Emma **HAMILTON** started out as a 'courtesan'.

The mythical idea that previous generations were **REPRESSED** feeds the modern myth that we now live in a 'garden of earthly delights'. (Foucault)

Culture changes by "interconnected mechanisms" and there has been a proliferation of possible sexualities and forms of **DESIRE**, "a deployment quite independent of the law".

Jimmy **SAVILE** sex abuse scandal (2016) and Harvey **WEINSTEIN**'s alleged abuse of power (2017) illustrate Foucault's argument in 1964 A History of Sexuality, as Foucault argues that power relations define how we see sex and sexuality – the powerful **SUBJUGATE** the weak and convince them of the benefits of compliance (the silence of Weinstein's victims is bought by money, jobs or intimidation).

Roger **SCRUTON** (Sexual Desire, 1986) rejects Foucault's claim that sexual morality is culturally **RELATIVE** and criticises Foucault for assuming that there could be societies in which a "problematisation" of the sexual did not occur.

"No history of thought could show the 'problematisation' of sexual experience to be peculiar to certain specific social formations: it is characteristic of personal experience generally, and therefore of every genuine social order". Roger Scruton, Sexual Desire

The fact that Leviticus chapter 18 defines a **PURITY CODE** which causes to stone to death adulterous women and homosexuals as evil doesn't mean that we don't have our own purity code (for example, found in the extreme disgust of paedophilia – a view different from the Greeks).

Gender as a Fluid Concept – Judith Butler (Gender Trouble 1990)

Christianity has encouraged society to impose a **BINARY** (two-sided) relation of women and men. This is then **IDEALISED** as a **HETEROSEXUA**L form, and in the ideal of a two parent family.

Feminists reject the idea that **BIOLOGY** is **DESTINY** (link this to the **TELEOLOGICAL** view of human identity in Natural Law) , but then develop an account of patriarchal culture which assumed that masculine and feminine genders would inevitably be built up from 'male' and 'female' bodies, making the same destiny just as inescapable.

Butler (1956-) argues (with Simone de Beauvoir) that gender is a **SOCIAL CONSTRUCT**. The idea is not fixed, but fluid. Gender is created by repetition of a type of **BODY LANGUAGE** and social attitudes to rebellion (such as disgust at cross-dressing). With Foucault she sees sex (male, female) as causing gender **STEREOTYPES** (masculine, feminine) which is seen to cause desire (towards the other gender).

'There is no gender identity behind the expressions of gender; ... identity is performatively constituted by the very "expressions" that are said to be its results.' (Judith Butler, Gender Trouble, p. 25)

PERFORMATIVITY of gender is a stylised repetition of acts, an imitation or miming of the dominant **CONVENTIONS** of gender. "The act that one does, the act that one performs is, in a sense, an act that's been going on before one arrived on the scene" (Gender Trouble).

"Gender is an impersonation and becoming gendered involves impersonating an ideal that nobody actually inhabits" (Judith Butler, interview with Liz Kotz in Artforum).

"Performativity has to do with **REPETITION**, very often the repetition of oppressive and painful gender norms" (Judith Butler, Gender Trouble).

Butler calls for **SUBVERSIVE ACTION** in the present: 'gender trouble' -- the mobilisation, subversive confusion, and proliferation of genders -- and therefore identity. She would approve of the transgender movement and its forms of direct action and protest in the UK.

Gender and Women's Liberation

PARADOX in a world of liberation and increased rights we still have the silence surrounding Savile and Weinstein, incidence of domestic and other violence against women, and the continued inequalities in pay and promotion in the workplace. Key dates include:

- **1885** Married women could keep hold of their wealth which previously passed to the husband, so restricting divorce.

- **1864** Contagious Diseases Act reacts to prevalence of venereal disease amongst the armed forces (30%) by permitting "policeman to arrest prostitutes in ports and army towns and bring them in to have compulsory checks for venereal disease. If the women were suffering from sexually transmitted diseases they were placed in a locked hospital until cured". **JOSEPHINE BUTLER** launches protest movement at the labelling and degrading of women.

- **1914-18** Women occupy many men's jobs in armaments factories, but in 1918 Unions insist they are made redundant to make way for returning men.

- **1918** Women over 30 obtain the vote after eight year suffragette struggle.

- **1928** Women over 21 obtain the vote.

- **1960s** the Pill allows women to regulate fertility, (Queen Victoria had eight children) experienced by both upper and lower classes.

- **1967** Abortion Reform Act allows termination up to 28 weeks if certain criteria fulfilled. Mental health criterion easily the most popular.

- **1969** Divorce Reform Act allows divorce for 'irretrievable breakdown' rather than just proof of adultery.

- **2004** Gender Recognition Act allows you to apply for a Gender recognition Certificate and so legally change gender after psychiatric assessment for gender dysphoria.

- **2014** Gay couples can be legally married (but not in church).

- **2017** Church of England issues transgender guidance for its 4,700 schools - "pupils need to be able to play with the many cloaks of identity' and should be able 'to explore the many possibilities of who they might be" including gay, lesbian and transgender. "Transphobic bullying causes damage and leads to mental health disorders", Archbishop of Canterbury.

- **2017** a A Bill to make gender identity a protected characteristic under the

Equality Act 2010 in place of gender reassignment and to make associated provision for transgender and other persons halted due to the election.

The Changing idea of Family

Comparing 2005 and 2015, we see a snapshot of a profound change in the concept of family continuing (from nuclear to reconstituted, and from **EXTENDED** to nuclear, and from two parent to one parent and from married to cohabiting).

You don't need to learn detailed statistics for A level.

However it may be worth knowing that the fastest growth has been in **COHABITING** couples followed by **LONE PARENT** families in the decade 2005-15. Married and civil partner families have not grown significantly in the ten year period. However, they are still the largest group overall at 8/19 million (42%). Only around a third of households have two people in them.

So we can say with confidence – families are much less likely to be presided over by a married couple than they were forty years ago – family life is far more **FRAGMENTED** and disparate (lone parent, reconstituted, gay or cohabiting, rather than married). Moreover there are many people of any gender living alone. There may be psychological and social **CONSEQUENCES** of these changes.

From 2014 gay people can legally get married – but overwhelmingly in non-religious services (gay couples can't get married in Church by church law). Gay marriages form a small proportion of total weddings – around 2%.

Christian views on Gender Roles

Augustine on Gender Roles

In Confessions Augustine list of the qualities of his mother Monica - patience, mildness, obedience, selfless service of others, temperance, piety, and even an aversion to gossip, are **STEREOTYPICAL** feminine virtues and vices.

He also describes his long-term relationship with a **CONCUBINE**. Women have one of two roles – mother or lover. Unlike Aquinas, Augustine sees men and women of equal rational capacity , but women by nature submissive because they are **WEAKER**.

Elaine Pagels's (1989) analyses of the cultural implications of the doctrine of **ORIGINAL SIN** , especially the role of the story of the Fall in Genesis 3. Pagels lays the blame for Christian sexual repression and misogyny (woman hatred) on Augustine, arguing that Augustine's pessimistic views of sexuality, politics, and human nature would come to dominate in Western culture, and that

"Adam, Eve, and the serpent—our ancestral story— would continue, often in some version of its Augustinian form, to affect our lives to the present day." (Elaine Pagels, Adam, Eve and the Serpent, page 34)

Aquinas on Gender Roles

Aquinas follows **ST PAUL** (1 Corinthians 11:10 "woman was created for the sake of man") in seeing women as **INTELLECTUALLY** inferior. Aquinas sees Ephesians 5:22 "the husband is head of the wife" by virtue of greater intellectual wisdom."Men are wiser and more discerning, and not so quickly taken in", he says.

In attempting to interpret **ARISTOTLE** Aquinas accepts his biological assertion that men are the **ACTIVE AGENT** in reproduction, and women the passive (submissive). It is part of **NATURAL LAW** that women are placed in submission to men – and have to obey men.

Luther (1483-1536) on Gender Roles

The creation of Adam and Eve is God's way of preventing human loneliness (**GENESIS 2**).

Adam and Eve were equals before God, and equally culpable in the **FALL**.

But (like Aquinas) Luther saw men as **SUPERIOR** and more guided by reason and destined to lead in life, and women destined to **SUBMIT.** Women had responsibilities for children and the home. The Lutheran view included equality in principle, but superiority and subordination in practice echoes the contradiction in **ST PAUL** (Galatians 3:28 'there is neither male nor female" versus Ephesians 5:22 "wives submit to your husbands").

Luther formulated the doctrine of three estates, which divided society into church, family and state each governed by a **PATRIARCHAL** household as their ideal, i.e. a structure in which the father exercised authority but was also a caring protector. But the **REFORMATION** picture overall is more ambiguous.

MELANCTHON (1497-1560) had theological discussions with highly intelligent women. Luther emphasised that a father performs a Christian act when washing his children's dirty nappies, for example. He also expressed his patriarchal respect for his own wife by calling her Mr Kathy.

Modern church on Gender Roles – Catholic, Liberal Protestant (USA)

The **EPISCOPALIAN** Church of America is the most **LIBERAL** of the Anglican communion of churches. They argue that gender matters because of language, imagery and power relations.

ESCHATOLOGICAL hope is for a future where gender ceases to matter – meantime we make small steps towards **JUSTICE** and **EQUALITY** for women.

"The expression of gender and sexuality are conditioned by culture and by experiences of oppression, especially as racial and ethnic diversity are considered" (Episcopalian Church, USA)

The structures of leadership, the language and the practices need to work together to transform the present.

In the Church of England, women priests were first ordained in **1993** and the first woman Bishop, Libby Lane, consecrated in **2015**. Currently there are 12/78 women Bishops (October 2017).

Christian Views on Social Changes

Linda **WOODHEAD** argues that a gap has opened up between Church Teaching and social attitudes on issues such as contraception and gay marriage. The church, faced with the challenge of **RELATIVISM,** has made increasingly tentative steps towards reform – and in the case of the **CATHOLIC** church, has held steadfastly in public to an orthodox (patriarchal) line.

So the increase in UK citizens identifying as **NO RELIGION** (in 2016 51%) does not equate to a lack of **SPIRITUALITY** but a rejection of orthodox forms of Christianity and the embracing of new forms of spirituality (such as New Age, meditation, mindfulness etc).

The Church of England continues to reject gay marriage in church, whilst taking a contradictory view on homosexual sex – gay priests must be celibate (but often in practice are not) whereas church members generally should be encouraged to be faithful to their partner.

In the Catholic church, research suggest only around 11% of Catholic women in the USA follow the prohibition on contraception and abortion, and 31% are on the pill – so fuelling allegations of **DOUBLE STANDARDS**. Meantime, in Africa **AIDS** infection remains endemic and safe sex officially discouraged by the Church.

CATHOLICS FOR CHOICE argues that "Abstinence before marriage and faithfulness in a marriage is beyond the realm of possibility here. The issue is to protect life. That must be our fundamental goal. African people must use condoms."

Christian Teaching – the Bible

Ephesians 5:22-33

EPHESIANS 5 needs to be interpreted in the context of a revolutionary document presented to a patriarchal culture. "The apostolic letters are addressed to people living in an environment marked by that same traditional way of thinking and acting". "All the reasons in favour of the "subjection" of woman to man in marriage must be understood in the sense of a "mutual subjection" of both "out of reverence for Christ". Mulieris Dignitatem p 24

Christian Teaching- Roman Catholic Mulieris Dignitatem (MD)

1971 Pope appoints commission to ensure "effective promotion of the dignity and the responsibility of women" culminates in 1988 in **MULIERIS DIGNITATEM** (of the vocation and dignity of women).

Reaffirms **IDEAL** of Mary as obedient and submissive handmaid of the Lord (Luke1:38), and pure virgin. Like Jesus himself, she is called to **SERVE**. She is the new **EVE** and the prototype of a **NEW CREATION**.

Also confirms the Creation order that "both man and woman are human beings to an equal degree, both are created in God's image". Genesis 1:28

Acknowledges the contradiction between two creation accounts (Genesis 1:28 versus Genesis 2:18-25). MD asserts, against traditional teaching, that

"The biblical text provides sufficient bases for recognising the essential equality of man and woman from the point of view of their humanity".

Word equality here does not mean 'equal rights' to exercise leadership in the church. Interpretation here is **RELATIONAL** and **TRINITARIAN**.

"Man - whether man or woman - is the only being among the creatures of the visible world that God the Creator "has willed for its own sake"; that creature is thus a person. Being a person means striving towards self-realisation (the Council text speaks of self-discovery), which can only be achieved "through a sincere gift of self". (Mulieris Dignitatem p16)

The model for this interpretation of the person is God himself as **TRINITY** (God in Three Persons) as a communion of Persons. To say that man is created in the **IMAGE** and likeness of God means that man is called to exist "for others, to become a gift", (Mulieris Dignitatem).

Affirms the feminine and masculine qualities of God eg "Can a woman forget her sucking child, that she should have no compassion on the son of her womb? Even these may forget, yet I will not forget you". (Isaiah 49:14-15).

The **FALL** 'obscures' and 'diminishes' the image of God but does not eliminate it. But consequences include pain (for women) and death for all. Man also 'shall have **DOMINION** (power) over women" (Genesis 3:16) as a part of the consequences of sin.

However, all 'unjust situations' should be remedied because the fundamental equality of Genesis 2 overrides the effects of the Fall in Genesis 3.

Gender differences need to be preserved as part of the **NATURAL CREATED**

ORDER. even the rightful opposition of women to what is expressed in the biblical words "He shall rule over you" (Genesis 3:16) must not under any condition lead to the "masculinisation" of women. In the name of liberation from male "domination", women must not appropriate to themselves male characteristics contrary to their own feminine "originality".

Despite evidence of a new relationship to women reflected in Jesus actions and teachings, and the presence of women as the first witnesses of resurrection , MD reaffirms that

"Virginity and motherhood are two particular dimensions of the fulfilment of the female personality". (Mulieris Dignitatem p 17).

MARY DALY would see the depiction of women as virgin, mother or whore as part of the conditioning of **PATRIARCHY** whereas **DAPHNE HAMPSON** would see the complex interpretations of Mulieris Dignitatem as part of the **IRREDUCIBLY** patriarchal nature of historical Christianity, the Bible and all its interpretations which justify inequality (such as the Catholic teaching against women priests and bishops).

Key Quotes

1. "One is not born, but rather one becomes a woman.. it is civilisation that produces this creature." Simone de Beauvoir.

2. "Gender is an impersonation . . . becoming gendered involves impersonating an ideal that nobody actually inhabits." Judith Butler, Gender Trouble

3. "My argument for the "moral significance" of gender is an extensive attack on the Kantian assumption behind modern feminism—the assumption that what I am essentially is a person, and that persons are essentially genderless." Roger Scruton, Sexual Desire

4. "According to Scruton's Aristotelian argument, love is to sexual desire as the mature flourishing life of a tree is to the young developing plant". Martha Nussbaum

5. "There is no gender identity behind the expressions of gender; ... identity is performatively constituted by the very "expressions" that are said to be its results." Judith Butler, Gender Trouble

6. "Even a pioneering feminist like Germaine Greer is forbidden to speak on campus lest her belief in real and objective sexual differences should threaten vulnerable students who have yet to decide which gender they are". Independent 3.11.17

7. "Within Christianity, more than in any other religion, women have had a special dignity, of which the New Testament shows us many important aspects." Pope Paul VI

Exam Questions

1. "Christians should resist current secular views of gender" Discuss

2. Evaluate the view that secular views of gender equality have undermined Christian gender roles

3. "Motherhood liberates rather than restricts". Discuss

4. Critically evaluate the view that idea of family is entirely culturally determined.

5. "Christianity follows where culture leads". Discuss

Further Reading

Tong, R. (2013) Feminist Thought, Routledge, Chapter 1

McGrath, A. (2010 5th Edition) A Christian Theology, Wiley-Blackwell, pages 88–89, 336–337

More A. Female Sexuality (Routledge, 2005) synopsis available on peped.org

Messer, N. (2006) SCM Study Guide to Christian Ethics, SCM Press, Chapter 8.

Mulieris Dignitatem, Roman Catholic Encyclical available on peped.org

Pagels, E. Adam, Eve and The Serpent (Vintage, 1989)

Ephesians 5:22–33 peped.org > Philosophy > christian-thought > feminism

Gender and Theology

Background

Paradoxically, Christianity presents itself as a prophetic movement of liberation and belief in a **NEW HEAVEN** and a **NEW EARTH** redeemed by the faithful. Mary **DALY** and Daphne **HAMPSON** are post-Christians feminists who reject the very basis of Christianity and the Christian God-concept. Rosemary **RUETHER** remains a Catholic calling the church to repent and change.

A word of warning though: Christianity isn't one entity and it is dangerous to **GENERALISE**. The **MONTANISTS** of the second to sixth century had women leaders and prophets, and the **QUAKERS** of the past 400 years have always followed a priestless equality where anyone can speak a word from God. Perhaps Christianity (following Emporer **CONSTANTINE**'s conversion in 316) have become too enmeshed in the power structures of many societies to be a prophetic movement and has become a rather laggardly reflection of its times.

Specification

A level requires that we study Ruether's discussion of the maleness of Christ and its implications for salvation including:

- Jesus' challenge to the male **WARRIOR MESSIAH** expectation

- God as the female **WISDOM** principle

- Jesus as the I**NCARNATION** of wisdom

Daly's claim that 'if God is male then the male is God' (1996:76) and its implications for Christianity, including:

- Christianity's 'Unholy Trinity' of rape, genocide and war
  - spirituality experienced through nature

Key terms

APOCRYPHA: That part of the Bible rejected by Protestant Christianity, but containing Wisdom literature which exalts the feminine.

ESCHATOLOGY: The end times, traditionally a time in the future when God judges the world. In feminism, eschatology is realized now with judgement on patriarchy and formation of a new society.

FEMINISM: A movement campaigning for the rights, empowerment and equality of women.

GENOCIDE: The attempt to eliminate a race or a religious group by extreme violence and murder

GOD/ESS: Ruether's genderless term for God

HERMENEUTICS: The study of methods of interpretation and the textual generation of meaning

INCARNATION: Embodiment of some value of goodness or aspect of God

MESSIAH: The 'anointed one' sent by God in fulfilment of Old Testament prophecy to liberate and redeem Israel

MONTANISM: prophetic movement in the second century where women prophesied and claimed visions directly from Christ.

PATRIARCHY: (Two Latin words, pater/arche) rule of the male. A form of society where men dominate, denigrate and oppress women.

SEXISM: Prejudice, stereotyping, or discrimination, typically against women, on the basis of sex.

SHEKINAH: The glory of God which traditionally shone forth from the altar, expelled by patriarchy and rediscovered in the Exodus community of women.

SPIRITUALITY: Response to the metaphysical reality beyond the physical, where the individual forms patterns of self-determination that build the common good.

Structure of Thought - Ruether

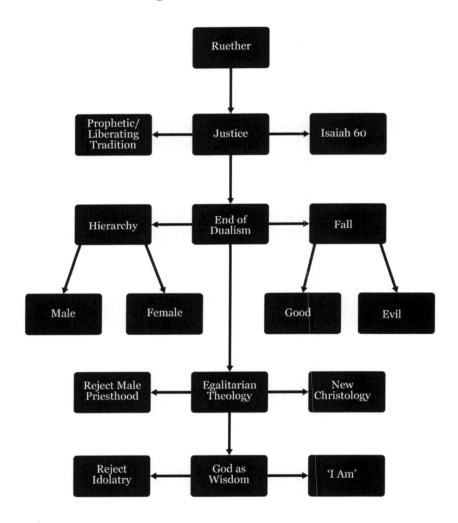

Hermeneutics of Suspicion

Paul **RICOEUR** (1913-2005) asks us to adopt a **HERMENEUTIC OF SUSPICION** when reading a text such as the Bible. We need to be suspicious of the **MOTIVES**, the **VALUES**, the culture of those who wrote it, and not just project our own values onto the text. James O'Donnell comments

"Liberation means, therefore, to opt for the exercise of an ideological suspicion in order to unmask the unconscious ideological structures which dominate and which favour a powerful, privileged minority." (O'Donnell 1982:32)

There is a **WORLD BEHIND** the text (the culture of Jesus' day) and there is a world **IN FRONT** of the text, our own culture. These **TWO HORIZONS** (Gadamer's term) need to merge in a valid interpretation that is **CRITICAL**.

Elizabeth Schüssler **FIORENZA** argues that theology is the product of each writer's experience and that this is determined by the historical and **SOCIAL CONTEXT** of every theologian. Theology is culturally conditioned and shapes, reflects, and serves a particular group's or individual's interests, (Fiorenza 1975:616).

Ruether argues that the Bible is riddled with **PATRIARCHY** and emerged from a world of hierarchy with males in charge. The **FEMININE** is constructed from these patriarchal values.

The social relationships are **ARCHAIC** and inappropriate for our time: they are reflected in a male clergy and a continued tolerance of **INJUSTICE** and **INEQUALITY**.

Behind the interpretation of the Bible lies the acceptance of **ARISTOTLE**'s biology that sees men and women as two separate classes of human and whereby

"The female is not only secondary to the male but lacks full human status in physical strength, moral self-control, and mental capacity. The lesser "nature" thus confirms the female's subjugation to the male as her "natural" place in the universe". (Ruether 1985:65)

Ruether's Hermeneutic

Controlling principle – whatever denigrates women is rejected, whatever builds up and values women is accepted. Then it is **EXPERIENCE** (rather than history) which is the starting-point of theology. The Bible needs to be interpreted anew, and the story of **REDEMPTION** retold in the light of women's experience. This may be linked to the **EXISTENTIAL** theology of Paul **TILLICH**.

There is a **PROPHETIC PRINCIPLE** in the Bible which can be rediscovered and brought to the fore: emphasising **JUSTICE** and the call to be a new people of **LIBERATION. ISAIAH 60** gives a radical vision of a just world order.

"God's Shekinah, Holy Wisdom, the Mother-face of God has fled from the high thrones of patriarchy and has gone into exodus with us". Ruether, 1985:87

The counter-culture of early Christianity which emphasised this were suppressed, for example, the female **PROPHETS** Priscilla and Maximilla in

MONTANISM. Priscilla claimed a night vision in which Christ slept by her side "in the form of woman, clad in a bright garment". She adopted a priestly ministry with direct voices and visions from God. Montanists were persecuted and ultimately suppressed with violence in the sixth century.

SEXISM is a sin against God/ess and against the fundamental golden thread of **JUSTICE** within the Bible.

"The dominant Christian tradition, if corrected by feminism, offers viable categories for interpreting human existence and building redemptive communities" Ruether, 1985:123

Ruether's God-Concept

GOD/ESS is the ground of all being. God is **GENDERLESS** and to turn God into the **MALE** is a form of **IDOLATRY** that serves men's interests.

In the **OLD TESTAMENT**, **YAHWEH** is the name of God – it means 'no name' or I **AM WHO I AM**.

Patriarchy encourages **HIERARCHY** with the idea of **TRANSCENDENCE**. Ruether emphasises **IMMANENCE** – God as **BEING** within all things.

Ruether sees God as **WISDOM** – the Greek word **LOGOS** and the idea in **WISDOM** literature (the Book of Wisdom is part of the **APOCRYPHA** – not in the Protestant Bible). **GOD/ESS** has sources in **PAGANISM**, and Babylonian **CREATION** myths – but the **MOTHER NATURE** idea was suppressed by the early Church.

LANGUAGE reflects patriarchal values – **FATHER**, Lord, King. "**OUR FATHER...THY KINGDOM COME**".

Can a Male Saviour Save?

Jesus' **GENDER** is irrelevant. Maleness of Christ has no **THEOLOGICAL** significance. The **MESSIAH** is an iconoclastic (idol-smashing) **PROPHET** in the tradition of **ISAIAH** or **AMOS**.

The real Jesus needs to be rediscovered and the Church should **REPENT** and cast off patriarchal values and images. Jesus is the I**NCARNATE WISDOM** of God (**LOGOS**, John 1).

Such a rediscovery embraces a new relation to the earth (link with Mary Daly's **GYN/ECOLOGY**). Feminism is, says Daly, **BIOPHILIC** (loves life). This creative thinking creates communities of liberation who engage in play of ideas. Ruether agrees.

The New Age and the Eschatological Community

Does not lie in the future, **ESCHATOLOGICALLY** as in patriarchal ideas – beyond the grave. Link with theological **IMMANENCE** (God is here now, the new community is realised here, now)

It is brought into being now in the **REDEEMED COMMUNITY – REALISED ESCHATOLOGY**.

Ruether believes church can be redeemed by forming new **BASE**

COMMUNITIES with **JUSTICE** at their heart. **CLERICALISM** (male priesthood) is a product of patriarchy and should be rejected.

Early Church experiments such as **MONTANISM** (2nd century) had women leaders: in Acts there is a prophetess, and Paul's argument "I do not allow women to have authority in the Church" (1 Corinthians) only makes sense in context of the rise of women **PROPHETS** in Corinth and discord that surrounded it.

Criticisms of Ruether

In a 1986 debate, Daphne Hampson makes three criticisms of Ruether's position (acronym **HIS**).

• **Historical** Roots of Christianity are Sexist. Ruether ignores the historically-entrenched nature of Christianity, which 'necessarily has one foot in the past'. Incarnation means that God became a human being at a particular time, within a patriarchal worldview. That Jesus only chose male apostles may be no accident. Hampson concludes that 'it cannot be the case that God is related in a particular way to a certain history'. Like Daly, Hampson is a post-Christian. Anthony Thiselton agrees:

"Some texts, by their very nature, draw part of their meaning from the actions, history and life with which they are inextricably interwoven"; Thiselton, New Horizons pg 66.

- **Incarnational** Doctrine is sexist. God 'sent his son'. Metaphors for God are male (with a few exceptions that are never developed). God calls Jesus 'My Beloved Son, whom I have chosen,' and asks Jesus' followers to 'listen to him' (Luke 9:35). Christian creeds ask us to affirm belief in "Jesus Christ, his only Son, our Lord'. Lord and Son are both patriarchal images.

- **Symbolic** world is sexist. The revelation of Christ in history is full of patriarchal symbols and messages. The Prodigal Son is having property divided between two men (Luke 15:11-35). The Good Samaritan is a male. When Jesus visits Martha and Mary, Mary is busy cooking and Martha commended for sitting passively at Jesus' feet, (Luke 1:38-42). Women who were Resurrection witnesses were not believed because the testimony of women is unreliable. Moreover, Paul is a Rabbi and retains some of the Levitical symbolic world of Rabbinic Judaism. Hampson points out 'we do not have stories of a man sitting at the feet of a female teacher'. When stories circulate in Corinth of women prophets, Paul seeks to suppress the upsurge by writing two letters to the Corinthians, both against women's liberation, insisting 'women keep silent in church' (1 Corinthians 14:34-5).

Hampson therefore accuses Ruether of misrepresenting the profoundly historical nature of Christian patriarchy, which still affects Christian theology and practice. Hampson is a **POST-CHRISTIAN**, Ruether a Christian **LIBERATION** theologian.

Structure of Thought - Mary Daly

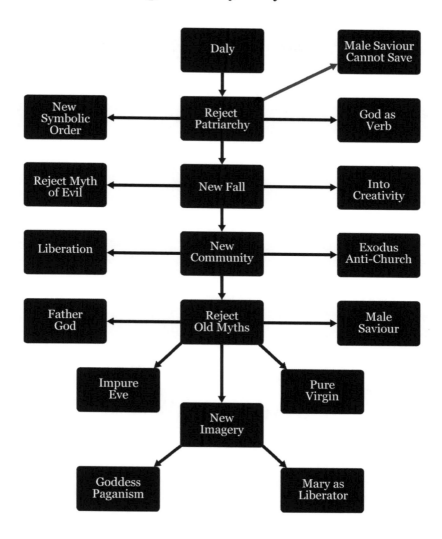

Background

Mary Daly (1928-2010) was a radical lesbian feminist theologian who taught at **BOSTON COLLEGE**. She almost always refused to let men into her classes, in 1999, a male student sued the school for discrimination. Daly was suspended and ultimately refused to comply. She also stated she found men disruptive. Lawrence Cunningham calls her 'the gold standard of **ABSOLUTE FEMINISM**."

The Myths that Bolster Patriarchy

Daly argues that male **MYTH-MAKERS** constructed an image of the feminine to mould women for their own purposes. The male is the **ROBBER** who robs women of "their myths, their energy, their divinity, their very selves". **PATRIARCHY** has 'stolen our **COSMOS** and turned it into Cosmopolitan magazine" and is the prevailing religion of the entire planet, whose essential message is **NECROPHILIA** (love of **DEATH** eg crucifixion and **MORTIFICATION** - putting our sins to death by self-flagellation).

She calls women to have the courage 'to see and to be' and represent the greatest challenge to the religions of the world. The ultimate **SIN** is patriarchal religion; yet women are **COMPLICIT** by living out the role of the submissive **OTHER**, represented in Christianity as **WEAK, OBEDIENT, DEPRAVED**. As in **AQUINAS**' thought, men are **SUPERIOR, WISE, STRONG, RATIONAL**.

The Patriarchal God

The language of the **FATHER** God legitimates male supremacy and oppression of women – "as God is male the male becomes god".

She rejects the God-image of Christianity in favour of participation in an **ULTIMATE REALITY** - a God-concept 'beyond and beneath'. The **IMAGE** of **GOD** is the creative potential in all human beings. In this **TRANSFORMATION** of symbols of God, God is transformed from a **NOUN** (**FATHER**, **LORD**) to a verb who is "form-destroying, form-creating, transforming power that makes all things new" (Daly, Beyond God the Father). God is **BEING** and **BECOMING**. We might describe this as a rejection of the Christian God and a rediscovery of earlier feminine god-concepts.

Myth of the Feminine

Daly accuses **AUGUSTINE** and **AQUINAS** of misogyny (women hatred) as they deny women the power to reach their full potential.

The male constructs the feminine as the originator of **EVIL** in the myth of the **FALL** and its interpretations. **EVE** is represented as the **SCAPEGOAT** of male sexual guilt. Daly encourages women to enter a new Fall - a **FALL** into **FREEDOM**, involving eating the forbidden fruit of **WISDOM** all over again. Two images of women: the **VIRGIN** and the **WHORE**, represented in the image of the **PURE VIRGIN MARY** and the fallen **MARY MAGDALENE**.

• **MARY** = the impossible virgin (still submissive to the will of the Father-God)

• **MARY MAGDALENE** (the fallen woman) = all other women cast in the image of the fallen **EVE**.

Daly calls women to stop playing the role of meek, subservient 'complement' to men, to re-imagine their power and renew the world.

Yet the virgin **MARY** can be adopted by feminism as a symbol of the **AUTONOMOUS** woman, the first woman to fall into **PARADISE**. Mary echoes back to a pre-Christian era of the **GREAT GODDESS**.

The Scapegoat Christ

Daly believes Jesus was simply a limited human being. It is **IDOLATRY** to suggest a **MALE** saviour can represent the eternal **BEING** which is God. Jesus is portrayed by patriarchy as the **SCAPEGOAT** for the sins originating in **EVE**, and the twin idealisations of **CHRIST** and **MARY** have nothing to do with history.

The projection of our evil onto these twin figures of **PURITY** results from an **INABILITY** to accept our own guilt. Feminism rejects the **SCAPEGOAT** Christ with its projections of **VICTIMHOOD** and the worship of the violence of the **CROSS** as part of the **NECROPHILIA** (love of **DEATH**) of patriarchy.

In the development of patriarchy, the male priest becomes the sole mediator controlling access to the deity. Women need to affirm **BIOPHILIA** (love of life).

A Fall into the Sacred

Women in exercising their **FREEDOM** and **POWER** fall into a new sacred space, a **SECOND COMING**, escaping the false **PARADISE** of patriarchal enslavement. They practise **BECOMING** by renouncing the traditional dichotomy of **HETEROSEXUAL/HOMOSEXUAL**, which are patriarchal classifications, to live in an environment that is "beyond, beneath and all around".

Women empowered cut loose from the **PSYCHOSEXUAL** chains that bind them to a patriarchal set of images, and a patriarchal power structure. Women are by nature **ANTI-CHURCH** with its over-emphasis on sexual and gender differences. Women have to 'live now the freedom we are fighting for', and **FEAR** and **GUILT** are no longer used as weapons of oppression. She calls both men and women to leave the church and become "an **EXODUS** community prepared to get on with the business of **LIVING**". Indeed men may understand the manipulation of **POWER** better as they see it from **WITHIN**.

"Male religion entombs women in sepulchres of silence in order to chant its own eternal and dreary dirge to a past that never was". Mary Daly, Beyond God the Father, page 145

Ultimately Daly believes in a new **COSMIC COVENANT** – which renounces the old order of meaningless desires, violence and war.

Gyn/Ecology

Daly plays on words to encourage women to 'weave tapestries of our own kind". She rages against the oppressive system in which "patriarchy is the homeland of males" and where they oppress and demonise women in rites of **SUTTEE** or **WITCH-BURNING**.

She analyses the **LANGUAGE** of patriarchy   and the mind/body/spirit **POLLUTION** this has brought about. **PHALLIC** myths predominate – from the Coca-Cola advert for the **REAL THING** to the Christian hymns glorying in the **DEATH** and real presence of Christ. With spiritual pollution comes pollution of the planet – as the male 'threatens to **TERMINATE** life on the planet through rape (of nature), genocide and war'.

"If life is to survive on this planet, there must be a decontamination of the Earth. I think this will be accompanied by an evolutionary process that will result in a drastic reduction of the population of males." (Gyn/Ecology page 54)

To escape the enslavement and **DENIGRATION** of the male, women need to invent a **NEW LANGUAGE** and set of social relations. Using **CREATIVE ANGER** and **BRILLIANT BRAVERY**, women rediscover 'our **WOMEN-LOVING** love". "We find our original Being and we SPIN our original **INTEGRITY**" and so put **POWER** and **JOY** back into living.

On contraception she comments, showing her playful use of language:

"It is obvious to Hags that few gynaecologists recommend to their heterosexual patients the most foolproof of solutions, namely Misterectomy. The Spinsters who propose this way by our be-ing, liv-ing, speak-ing can do so with power precisely because we are not preoccupied with ways to get off the heterosexually defined contraceptive dilemma." (Gyn/Ecology p.239)

Criticisms of Daly

- Black theologian Audrew Lourde criticised Daly for refusing to acknowledge the '**HERSTORY** and myth' of women of colour. The severe oppression they have suffered greatly outweighs the discrimination of white women. There's a racial bias to Daly's work and a racist indifference to the plight of minorities who suffer greatest oppression.

- Patriarchy cannot assist in explaining why only a few men in a patriarchy use violence against women and why many males have campaigned for women's rights over the centuries (the first man being Jesus himself who overthrew aspects of anti-women purity code of **LEVITICUS**).

- Daly wanted **WOMEN** to rule men and was herself a lesbian and vegetarian. "I really don't care about men" she commented in an interview. Yet isn't this perpetuating the **DUALISM** she herself rejects as oppressive?

- The **FRAMEWORK** of Patriarchy is assumed in all instances. There is no other explanation given for witch-burning (Christian) or suttee (Hindu). Paradoxically, Enlightenment enquiry provoked an upsurge of interest in alchemy and other forms of magic: it is arguably the flip-side of the stress on autonomous reason. James I wrote a book on witches.

- People who criticise her thesis are described as "**FEMBOTS** doing Daddy's work".

- No analysis of class, wealth or race as instruments of oppression of women.

Confusions to Avoid

1. **Feminists cannot be Christians**. Feminists like Ruether argue that Christianity can be restored to a lost **PROPHETIC** movement, transforming society, but only if patriarchy is rejected. A male saviour is irrelevant to salvation and the male perspective is a gloss overlaying the true gospel, which can be reconstructed as a gospel of liberation and hope. However, both Daphne Hampson and Mary Daly call women out of the church and see Christianity as irredeemably patriarchal. They are post-Christian feminists.

2. **The Church has no response to feminism**. This isn't a fair assessment because the Protestant churches have reformed themselves and allowed women priests and bishops (where appropriate to their order of ministry). The Church of England ordained women **PRIESTS** in 1993 and women **BISHOPS** in 2013. The Roman Catholic Church produced a brave apologetic for its position in not allowing women priests and bishops in Mulieris Dignitatem, which lay great emphasis on the equality of the sexes, but failed to reconcile the **CONTRADICTION** in the Bible between the Paul of Galatians (there is neither male nor female) and the Paul of Ephesians and Corinthians (wives obey your husbands, and "I do not allow women to have authority over a man') . Moreover, the Catholic persistence in advocating the **RHYTHM** method of contraception suggests that the **AUTONOMY** of women and their right to choose is still being overridden by the male perspective.

3. **A male saviour cannot save**. This extreme position, taken by Mary Daly, would appear to overlook the revolutionary attitude of Jesus towards women whom he included in his inner circle and addressed as equals – "daughter, your faith has made you well, go in peace" (Mark 5). Arguably when Jesus 'emptied himself taking the form of a servant' (Philippians 2:7), he also gave up the genderless **INFINITY** of God (Yahweh – means 'I am who I am'). God cannot have a gender and so if Jesus is one with God his gender must be irrelevant for salvation. Messiah is a genderless idea. Emphasis on the gender of Christ and the virginity of Mary comes later as the male-dominated church hierarchy produces creeds which impose uniformity on belief and cast out so-called heretics, such as the **MONTANISTS**.

Possible Exam Questions

1. 'A male saviour cannot save'. Discuss with reference to the theologies of Rosemary Ruether and Mary Daly.

2. "If God is male the male is God'. Discuss

3. Critically contrast the theologies of Ruether and Daly.

4. "The Church is irrevocably patriarchal'. Discuss

5. "God is genderless, and so the idea of the Father-God is idolatry". Discuss

6. "Only a spirituality of women can save the planet from environmental degradation and war'. Discuss

Reading

Listen to Mary Daly interview
https://archive.org/details/KDVS_The_Fringe_4-5-06

Mary Daly, Beyond God the Father, (Beacon, 1992)

Mary Daly, Can a Male Saviour Save? (Select 'Extracts' from:
http://peped.org/philosophicalinvestigations/christian-thought/feminism/)

Elisabeth Schussler Fiorenza, Sharing Her Word (T & T Clarke, 1998)

Daphne Hampson, After Christianity (SCM, 2002)

Rosemary Ruether, Sexism and God-talk (Beacon, 1993)

Bible Passages such as 2 Corinthians 11:3 and 1 Tim 2:14 became the argument for the subordination of women and Mark 5 and John 8 for Jesus' more liberating attitudes to women. Isaiah 60 gives the prophetic call for justice. Paul in Galatians 3:16 seems to contradict Ephesians 5. Can they be reconciled?

Hampson, (After Christianity, 2002), states that if Christianity is true, God cannot be thought of as moral or good "given the harm that this myth has done to women" (Hampson 2002: xv). The Christian myth is misogynistic (Hampson 2002: xvi) and morally suspect (Hampson 2002: vxiii).

Postscript

Peter Baron read Politics, Philosophy and Economics at New College, Oxford and afterwards obtained an MLitt for a research degree in Hermeneutics at Newcastle University. He qualified as an Economics teacher in 1982, and taught ethics at Wells Cathedral School in Somerset from 2006-2012. He is currently a freelance writer and speaker.

Daniella Dunsmore trained in Theology at Cambridge University. She is currently subject leader in Religious Studies at Thetford Grammar School, speaks at Conferences, and is a Teach First Ambassador.

In 2007 we set up a philosophy and ethics community dedicated to enlarging the teaching of philosophy in schools by applying the theory of multiple intelligences to the analysis of philosophical and ethical problems. So far over 700 schools have joined the community and over 30,000 individuals use his website every month.

To join the community please register your interest by filling in your details on the form on the website. We welcome contributions and suggestions so that our community continues to flourish and expand.

www.peped.org contains **EXTRACTS** and **FURTHER READING** mentioned in the exam specification, plus additional articles, handouts and essay plans. Notice that the exam specification merely gives guidance as to further reading - you may use any source or philosopher you find relevant to the construction of your argument. Indeed, if you have the courage to abandon the selection (and any examples) introduced by your textbook, you will relieve the examiner of boredom and arguably launch yourself on an A grade trajectory.

Printed in Great Britain
by Amazon